Talking,
Listening,
and
Teaching

Talking, Listening, and Teaching

and

Teaching

A Guide to
**Classroom
Communication**

Thomas S. C. Farrell

Skyhorse Publishing, Inc.

Copyright © 2009 by Corwin Press.
First Skyhorse Publishing edition 2018

All rights reserved. No part of this book may be reproduced in any manner without the express written consent of the publisher, except in the case of brief excerpts in critical reviews or articles. All inquiries should be addressed to Skyhorse Publishing, 307 West 36th Street, 11th Floor, New York, NY 10018.

Skyhorse Publishing books may be purchased in bulk at special discounts for sales promotion, corporate gifts, fund-raising, or educational purposes. Special editions can also be created to specifications. For details, contact the Special Sales Department, Sky Pony Press, 307 West 36th Street, 11th Floor, New York, NY 10018 or info@skyhorsepublishing.com.

Skyhorse® and Skyhorse Publishing® are registered trademark of Skyhorse Publishing, Inc.®, a Delaware corporation.

Visit our website at www.skyhorsepublishing.com.

10 9 8 7 6 5 4 3 2 1

Library of Congress Cataloging-in-Publication Data is available on file.

Cover design by Rose Storey

Print ISBN: 978-1-51073-299-5
Ebook ISBN: 978-1-51073-305-3

Printed in the United States of America

Contents

Preface   vii

Acknowledgments   ix

About the Author   xi

1. *Talking, Listening, Teaching:*
   Understanding Classroom Communication   1
   Mary's Class: An Illustration   1
   What Is Communication?   5
   What Is Classroom Communication?   7
   Talking and Listening   8
   A Framework for Understanding
      Classroom Communication   10
   Studying Communication Patterns   13
   Reflecting on Classroom Communication   15

2. *I Treat Them All the Same:*
   Exploring Classroom Communicative Competence   17
   "I Treat Them All the Same"   18
   What Is Classroom Communicative
      and Interactional Competence?   19
   Home and School Communication Differences   21
   Gender Differentiation   24
   Communication Apprehension   25
   Reflecting on Classroom Communicative Competence   26

3. *You Talk Like a Teacher:* **Collecting
   and Analyzing Classroom Communication**   27
   Basic Classroom Communication Structure   28
   Variability in Classroom Communication Structure   29
   How to Examine Classroom Communication Patterns   31
   Reflecting on Classroom Communication Data   36

4. *Why Don't They Do What I Ask?*
   Developing Effective Classroom Participation   37
   A Bad Beginning   37
   Organizing Effective Classroom Participation   41
   Teacher Talk   44
   Reflecting on Effective Classroom Participation   47

5. *What Is 2 + 2?* **Examining Teachers' Questions**   49
   Informant Questioning Strategies   50
   Types of Teacher Questions   52
   Ways of Directing Questions   55
   Characteristics of Good Teacher Questions   56
   Characteristics of Unproductive Questions   57
   Teacher Wait-Time   58
   Reflecting on Teachers' Questions   60

6. *OK! Good!* **Exploring Teacher Feedback**   61
   Purposes of Teacher Feedback   62
   Teacher Feedback Strategies   63
   Reflecting on Teacher Feedback   68

7. *Two Heads Are Better Than One:*
   Utilizing Learner Groupings   69
   Whole-Class Grouping   70
   Turn Allocation in Whole-Class Grouping   71
   Small Groups/Pair Work   75
   Making Groups Work   77
   Reflecting on Learner Groupings   80

8. *I See What You're Saying:* **Recognizing**
   Nonverbal Communication in the Classroom   81
   Functions of Nonverbal Communication   82
   Types of Nonverbal Communication   83
   Teachers' Use of Nonverbal Behaviors in the Classroom   88
   Reflecting on Nonverbal Communication   90

9. *Professional Development:* **Reflecting**
   on Classroom Communication and Interaction   91
   Reflective Practice as Professional Development   92
   Thinking About Your Own Classroom   95
   Reflecting on Classroom Communication and Interaction   97

References   99

Index   103

Preface

For many years now, teachers of all levels of experience and in all subject areas have been encouraged to reflect on every aspect of their teaching. Surprisingly, however, one aspect of reflection that has been neglected is classroom communication and how it influences learning, both positively and negatively. Classroom communication differs from everyday communication in that its main purpose is to instruct and inform. A classroom is a small society with its own values, rules, and language, and teachers use language (both verbal and non-verbal) as the main way of communicating with their students for both instructional and social purposes during classroom lessons. Although classroom communication is highly regulated and ritualized, many teachers, students, and administrators seem unaware of the different ways classroom communication provides, or blocks, opportunities for students to reach optimum levels of learning. In addition, teachers may not know how to investigate the different communication patterns that exist in their classrooms. The purpose of *Talking, Listening, and Teaching: A Teacher's Guide to Classroom Communication* is to encourage teachers, students, and administrators to examine and reflect systematically on classroom communication and interaction and their implications for student learning.

This book is designed to serve teachers who are interested in pursuing professional development either alone, with a friend, or in teacher study groups. It can be used as a textbook for inservice teacher development courses as well as for teacher preparation courses in such disciplines as Education, Communication Studies, and Teaching English as a Second Language.

Each of the nine chapters in this book will help teachers systematically uncover various aspects of classroom communication and interaction. Chapter 1 outlines and discusses what classroom communication is and offers an overall framework that teachers can use to understand classroom communication and interaction. Chapter 2 asks teachers to reflect on how they view their students' competence in classroom communication and interaction, with considerations for gender and communication apprehension, as well as for sociocultural and linguistic backgrounds. Chapter 3 outlines how teachers can investigate classroom communication and shows them how to collect, examine, and analyze classroom communication. Chapter 4 discusses how teachers can organize classroom communication so that their students can participate in classroom activities and events effectively. Chapter 5 examines teachers' use of questions and discusses the characteristics of productive and unproductive questions and how long teachers should wait for answers after asking a question. Chapter 6 looks at teacher feedback and discusses how teachers can use effective feedback strategies. Chapter 7 explores the use and abuse of group work and shows teachers how they can make group work more effective. Chapter 8 explores nonverbal communication in the classroom and outlines how teachers can become more aware of the different types of nonverbal communication and their effect on student learning. Chapter 9, the final chapter, discusses how teachers can make reflecting on classroom communication and interaction part of their overall professional development by suggesting ways individual teachers or teachers in groups can examine different aspects of classroom communication and interaction.

Readers can start their reflections with any chapter and pursue them in as much detail as their schedules permit. One of the unique features of this book is the section in each chapter called "Thinking About Your Own Classroom," which includes provocative questions to help teachers directly apply the material they have read to their own classroom context. Teachers can, of course, think about their class on their own or with other teachers, or they can make up their own questions for discussion. Just as Socrates said that the unexamined life is not worth living, I suggest that the unexamined class is not worth teaching. I hope that teachers, students, and administrators get as much fun out of reading this book as I have had in writing it. Happy reflecting!

Acknowledgments

N o book can be written solely by any author, and this one is no exception. I would like to acknowledge all the educators and students who have influenced my thoughts over the years on the general topic of reflection and specifically on reflecting on classroom communication and interaction. As always, I want to thank my wife, Mija, and my daughters, Sarah and Ann, who must put up with me as I write. I would also like to thank Carol Collins from Corwin both for her constant encouragement and mentoring as I wrote the manuscript and for introducing me to Susan Liddicoat, who really put the polish on the contents of this book.

Corwin gratefully acknowledges the contributions of the following reviewers:

Melissa Albright, Sixth Grade Communication Arts Teacher
Springfield R-XII School District, Springfield, MO

Kara Coglianese, Director of Learning
Wheeling School District 21, Wheeling, IL

Sara Coleman, Chemistry Instructor
Norwalk High School, Norwalk, IA

Carrice Cummins, Associate Professor
Louisiana Tech University, Ruston, LA

About the Author

 **Thomas S. C. Farrell** is a professor of Applied Linguistics at Brock University, Canada. His professional interests include reflective practice and language-teacher education and development. He is the series editor for the Language Teacher Research series (Asia, Americas, Africa, Australia/New Zealand, Europe, and the Middle East) for TESOL, USA. His recent books are *Succeeding With English Language Learners: A Guide for Beginning Teachers* (2006, Corwin); *What Successful Literacy Teachers Do: 70 Research-Based Strategies for Teachers, Reading Coaches, and Instructional Planners* (2007, coauthored with Neal Glasgow, Corwin); *Reflective Language Teaching: From Research to Practice* (2008, Continuum Press); and *Teaching Reading to English Language Learners: A Reflective Guide* (2009, Corwin).

CHAPTER ONE

Talking, Listening, Teaching

Understanding Classroom Communication

People communicate in various formal and informal settings, from making a presentation in a business meeting to chatting at a cocktail party. These settings are familiar to us, and we think we know how to communicate in both situations; however, we also encounter other settings in which we must communicate in a more ritualized manner, such as in a court of law or in a classroom. Ah! But you say, since we all went to school, we are all familiar with classrooms and know how to communicate in them. That is the problem for teachers: we teachers take this knowledge of communicating in classrooms for granted and assume *all* children who enter our classrooms also know how to communicate effectively. We also assume that, as teachers, our communications in our classes are always clear and foster an effective learning environment. I beg to differ, and that is why I wrote this book on classroom communication. To illustrate, let's consider a class where I observed and transcribed a classroom communication.

MARY'S CLASS: AN ILLUSTRATION

Mary, a fifth-grade teacher, is about to begin her class. What follows is the opening (the first 21 turns) of the reading lesson in which she is trying to get the students ready for the main topic: reading fantasy books.

Turns

1: Mary: OK, remember we were talking about some of the characters you can find in fantasy books. OK, I'm sure some of you have read, OK. Fantasy books which include . . . can you name me some of the characters you can find in fantasy books or stories? Anyone?

2: Student 1: Witch.

3: Mary: A witch. Very good.

4: Student 2: Red Riding Hood.

5: Mary: Is Red Riding Hood a fantasy? Red Riding Hood is a . . .

6: Student 2: Fairy tale.

7: Mary: Very good. Red Riding Hood is a fairy tale. We are talking about witches, OK.

8: Student 3: Dragon.

9: Mary: Dragon. Very good.

10: Student 4: Goblin.

11: Mary: Goblin. Yes.

12: Student 5: Elf.

13: Mary: Elf and dwarf? Excellent! Anyone else know anymore?

14: Student 6: Knights.

15: Mary: Knights! Yes! Right, OK now, look at the pictures on page 80. Today, we are going to learn some words, OK, that we can find in reading books. What words can you see? Please write them on the page.

[Students work alone.]

[Mary notices that John is not doing anything, so Mary goes to his desk.]

16: Mary: Is everything OK? Is anything the matter?

17: John:	*[Silence]*	
18: Mary:	You aren't doing your work. Are you sick?	
19: John:	*[Silence]*	
20: Mary:	If you do not join in, I will have to ask you to stay after class.	
21: John:	*[John gets up and leaves the class.]*	

[After class, Mary reports John to the vice-principal.]

The first 15 turns of this episode show us that the lesson was probably a typical one for Mary in terms of encouraging her students to read on their own during class time. However, around Turn 11 (although this is not indicated in the transcript until after Turn 15), she noticed that one of her students, John, an African-American student, was not reacting to any of her questions and was just sitting silently at his desk with his arms folded. After Turn 15, when all the students started to work alone, Mary went over to John. After this incident (when John walked out), Mary reported John to the vice-principal and said that he had disrupted her class and should be disciplined. In fact, Mary demanded that the vice-principal talk to John's parents because this was not the first time John had remained silent and unwilling to answer her questions. Many teachers may sympathize with Mary because, on the surface, it can be perceived that John was not a willing participant in her class and was not willing to communicate directly with her when she asked him questions. Mary even told the vice-principal that John was one of the very few students in her class who acted like this; he also happened to be the only African-American in her class.

Behind the Scene: The Real Story

When we examine all the issues in this example, we see that there is much more here than meets the eye in terms of what we take for granted in our classroom communication. One of the first issues we must consider here is that John is the only African-American student in Mary's class. It may be the norm in John's cultural background (African-American) not to respond to "wh" questions, and silence may be appropriate when being spoken to by an adult. In other words, John's unwillingness to talk during classroom events may have been a direct result of the different verbal conventions in his home community and those of the school community. John is from a cultural background that suggests that communication is more implied than direct and where explicit verbal messages are not necessary for understanding. Mary is from a cultural background where groups require communication to be detailed and explicit, and as such, Mary became frustrated with John because his communication is indirect and even circular. What this example shows is that the interpersonal relationship between the teacher and the student has an impact (dramatic in this case) on what happens in the classroom and that differences in and a lack of awareness of different communication styles can lead to misunderstandings. As Powell and Caseau (2004) suggested, "The further students depart from these communication conventions, the more at risk they become" (p. 47).

Thus, teachers must realize that many communities differ from the ways of talking expected in the school, and they must be ready to make allowances for such differences. When these differences are noticed, teachers should try to maximize their students' knowledge and uses of language in the classroom. For example, it would have been helpful for Mary to know about Heath's (1983) study of the different ways of talking and interacting in an African-American community and in two other communities, one of which included a mostly white, middle-class, school-oriented community (see Chapter 2). Mary would have learned that in the African-American community (called Trackton), parents did not use questioning as a mode of interaction with children at home and children were not expected to be information givers or even conversation partners for adults. So when teachers from a European-American background (like Mary) asked questions of their classes that they knew the answer to (labeled *display questions*—see Chapter 5 for more information), the African-American students did not respond because they had never heard that mode of interaction at home. Of course, the teachers perceived that the students from Trackton were being uncooperative, and even unwilling to participate in classroom activities, and gave them lower grades. Heath and her researchers decided to intervene and tried to make the teachers aware of their question types and their effect on the African-American students; they tried to get them to ask more open-ended questions that the students would have been more comfortable answering. Then they attempted to show and explain to the African-American students the types of questions the European-American teachers used (from a tape recording) so that they could understand them better. In this way, both sides of the communication desk (the teacher and the students, who may have different home communication conventions) can come to a greater understanding of what it means to be communicatively competent in each lesson (see Chapter 2 for more discussion on classroom communicative competence). Teachers tend to have idealized forms (or *schemata*) of classroom communicative competence, or the ways students should participate in their classes, but we should realize that children may not have built up these same schemata—they tend to develop gradually and, as such, must be learned so all students can participate fully in our classes. In other words, clear and consistent lessons may allow all students to attend to lesson content more than lesson procedure and may decrease the stress they experience as they adapt to this new environment. When we really examine the communication and interaction patterns in Mary's class, we can understand how an awareness of the way classroom communication is set up and develops can help teachers better facilitate learning in their classes. This chapter outlines some principles of communication, the nature of classroom communication, and what makes it unique. The chapter also offers a framework for novice and experienced teachers to help them reflect on and manage classroom communication and interaction in today's complex classrooms.

WHAT IS COMMUNICATION?

To begin, we need to define the terms that will form the basis of our discussion. The term *communication* is used frequently in modern times, but what do we actually mean by this term? There are more than 126 different definitions of communication (Civikly, 1992), and of course, this has resulted in a certain amount of confusion as to the meaning of this term. For example, communication can mean *a process of interaction, a discipline of study,* or even *an electronic media system.* However, for the purposes of this book, we will be looking at communication as a process; that is, the *process* of communication in the classroom that involves a "sorting, selecting, and sending of symbols in such a way as to help a listener find in his or her own mind a meaning or response similar to that intended by the communicator" (Ross, 1978, p. 21).

A useful starting point for teachers who are interested in reflecting on classroom communication patterns is this list of six principles of communication (adapted from Civikly, 1992):

1. *Communication is a process in constant change.* This first principle points out that communication is changing all the time.

2. *Communication is a system of rules.* Even though communication is constantly changing, it also has rules (which differ depending on the context—see Principle 6 below) that are usually only noticed when they are violated.

3. *Communication messages are both verbal and nonverbal.* Whenever we speak, we are sending both a verbal and a nonverbal message. Part of communication in classrooms is nonverbal, for the way we express our verbal message often tells a listener how to interpret it. Abercrombie (1968) correctly pointed out: "We speak with our vocal organs, but we converse with our entire bodies. Conversation consists of much more than a simple interchange of spoken words" (p. 55). Nonverbal communication in the classroom will be discussed in more detail in Chapter 8.

4. *Communication is transactional.* As the title of this book (and this chapter) suggests, when we are teaching *and* talking, we are also trying to understand our students' behaviors, facial expressions, and speech, just as they are also listening to us and trying to understand our actions and reactions.

5. *The communication process involves mutual influence.* Following from the transactional view of communication (see Principle 4), we note that how others are responding to us affects how we act and react. We may adjust our teaching actions depending on the level of our awareness; we may speed up, slow down, repeat, ask for a clarification, or make other such adjustments.

6. *Communication occurs in a context that influences the process of communication.* This principle of communication emphasizes the role of context as an influencing force on an interaction. The context is described broadly as the surroundings in which the interaction takes place. For our purposes, the context of communication is the classroom, which has a huge impact on the type of communication that occurs.

THINKING ABOUT YOUR OWN CLASSROOM

- Do you think the patterns of communication that exist in your classroom are providing maximum opportunities for your students to learn? If so, how do you know, and what evidence do you have to back up your claims?
- How do you monitor communication and interaction in your classes?
- How and how often do you monitor your use of language in your teaching?
- What is your opinion of the six principles outlined above? Do you disagree with any? Can you add any more to this list?
- What is your understanding of Principle 4, which states that communication is transactional?

WHAT IS CLASSROOM COMMUNICATION?

I know that what a classroom is may seem obvious to all teachers, but I think it best to define what it is so we all know what we mean when we use this word. Tsui (1995) defined the classroom as a "place where more than two people gather together for the purpose of learning, with one having the role of teacher" (p. 1). I like this definition because it contains two important pieces of information: learning is supposed to take place (the reason for the classroom) and one of the participants takes responsibility for ensuring that this learning will take place (the teacher).

What do we now mean by classroom communication? Classroom communication includes the face-to-face interactions and the communications necessary between the participants involved in the classroom to ensure that learning takes place. As Briscoe, Arriaza, and Henze (2009) suggested, it is within these face-to-face interactions that teachers use language to "communicate their expectations of students, faculty, and parents; to discuss policies, praise people, propose changes in curriculum, indicate that they are listening, carry out disciplinary action, and for a host of other actions" (p. 16). That is one of the ways classroom communication differs from normal communication in the community—the main purpose of communication in a classroom is to instruct and inform. In addition, communication in a classroom setting is unique because it has highly regulated patterns of communication between teachers and students, both of whom have a different status (the teacher has the higher status in the classroom if not in society as a whole). These same roles are not present in any other communication events or settings in society (the closest would be in a court of law or in a psychiatrist's office). The higher status of the teacher allows him or her to conduct the class from beginning to end; he or she can choose the topic, decide how to divide the topic into smaller units, control who talks, and when and where they do so. This does not happen in other normal conversations, such as at a cocktail party where topic changes are unpredictable and uncontrollable (although Chapter 3 will point out that many of our friends who are not teachers may think that we *do* try to control both the topic and when and who talks). So teachers, whether consciously or not, communicate (usually by using language) in order to orchestrate learning events in their classroom. Mercer (1995) suggested that teachers use communication in the classrooms in order to accomplish three things:

1. *To elicit relevant knowledge from students,* so that teachers can see what the students already know and understand and so that the knowledge is seen to be "owned" by students as well as teachers.

2. *To respond to things that students say,* not only so that students get feedback on their attempts but also so that the teacher can incorporate what students say. Teachers can respond to what students say through the use of *confirmations, repetitions, clarifications, elaborations,* and *reformulations.* (These terms will be discussed later in the book.)

3. *To describe the classroom experiences that they share with students.* Mercer (1995) made the argument that "to be effective, any teacher needs to explore the scope of a learner's existing knowledge" (p. 10), and this is achieved through such communication and talk techniques as *eliciting, responding,* and *describing: eliciting* knowledge from the students, *responding* to what the students say, and *describing* the classroom experiences that they both share.

TALKING AND LISTENING

Teachers use *talking* in classrooms as their main communication device, and as Mercer (1995) suggested, it is really through a teacher's response to communication and interaction that meaning can be created and then shared by all the participants. Much of the remainder of the contents of this book assume that the type of communication that teachers use in their classrooms is mostly in the form of talk, except for the final chapters that discusses how teachers use different forms of nonverbal communication in their classrooms. But in fact, we teachers talk *and* listen at the same time, and as we teach, we also look at our students' behaviors, facial expressions, and speech (while at the same time our students are also attempting to understand our behaviors, expressions, and speech).

When I talk about a teacher listening, I like to emphasize an *active* form of listening where teachers show their students that they are really listening. Such active listening can be achieved by teachers who follow a sequence of interactions in which the teacher as listener restates what the student has said and, through further comments and questions, helps the student clarify any specific issues of concern she or he may have.

Another means of verifying a listener's understanding of a message is called the *perception check* (Brophy & Good, 1991). For example, a student might ask his teacher, "Why do I have to go to gym?" The teacher's questions may help to find out the concerns behind this question. It could be that the student does not feel well, is self-conscious about his or her body, is afraid of the coach, or may be worried about a test after gym class and wants to use the time to study. According to Brophy and Good, when using a perception check, the teacher first states what he or she has heard and interpreted as the student's concern and then asks the student if that interpretation is accurate.

Students also provide certain signals of listening and comprehension failure when trying to understand the teacher. For example, students can use the following (adapted from Brophy & Good, 1991):

- A *focused/directive* strategy, where the student provides specific information to the teacher about what he or she does not understand and then asks for some type of clarification. For example, "Do you mean that *X* assumes change?"
- A *focused/nondirective* strategy, where the student provides specific information about what he or she does not understand but does not request any clarification. For example, "I don't understand the difference between a common future and a common goal."

- A *personally qualified* strategy, where the student's response takes the form of "mazes of questions/ideas" (p. 38) that the teacher must work through in order to respond. For example, "How is what she said different from what I said? . . . That's what I meant to say, so maybe I just didn't say it right."

THINKING ABOUT YOUR OWN CLASSROOM

- What does active listening mean to you?
- How do you show you are really listening to the students in your classroom?
- How do students show they are listening to you in your classroom?

A FRAMEWORK FOR UNDERSTANDING CLASSROOM COMMUNICATION

This book looks at *how* and *why* patterns of communication are established and maintained in classrooms. The chapters are all based on a framework for understanding communication in classrooms adapted from the work of Hugh Mehan (1979) and Douglas Barnes (1976). I am influenced by Mehan's (1979) work because he suggested that the classroom is a unique environment because it is the teacher who decides the speaking rights within a classroom as he or she holds all the authority and all the rights to speak and no other person in the room has the right to object. This, he said, affects the underlying communication structure of classroom communication depending on how the teacher wants to distribute these rights to the students on when, how, and why they are to speak. In a descriptive study of a first-grade classroom in the United States, Mehan used two types of units of analysis to describe teacher and student face-to-face verbal interaction: an *elicitation act* consisting of the teacher's inquiry (an I), followed by the student's response (an R), and the teacher evaluation (an E). In addition, Mehan (1979) identified four categories of teachers' elicitations (I):

- *Choice elicitations,* which call on students to agree or disagree with the teacher's inquiry, or choose one from a set of alternatives

- *Product elicitations,* which ask students to provide a factual response
- *Process elicitations,* which call for students to give an opinion or interpretation
- *Metaprocess elicitations,* where students are asked to explain their reasoning

This classic *IRE* sequence was changed slightly in the United Kingdom by the work of Sinclair and Coulthard (1975), who suggested that the lesson consists of *exchanges* and said "the typical exchange in the classroom consists of an *initiation,* followed by a *response,* from the pupil, followed by *feedback,* to the pupil's response from the teacher" (p. 3), or *IRF.* I use Mehan's (1979) *IRE* sequence as the usual underlying communication structure for most classrooms that operate within three broad phases: an *opening phase* to orient students, an *instructional phase,* and a *closing phase.* The opening and closing phases will vary from teacher to teacher with the use of informatives and directives; however, the instructional phase is a joint production between the teacher and the students in the form of an *initiation, response/reply,* and an *evaluation/feedback,* as outlined in the beginning of this section (see Chapter 3 for more of Mehan's ideas).

Barnes's (1976) classic work on classroom communication and interaction suggested that patterns of classroom communication are established and maintained by teachers, and these determine not only the ways in which our students react and respond but also heavily influence what our students ultimately learn. Most important, it is teachers and students *together* who attempt to interpret classroom communications and activities through their *own* frames of reference, and if these frames are different, then there are likely to be outcomes that are different from what was anticipated by both teachers and students. So the framework that is presented in this book maintains that classroom learning is really a negotiation between teachers' *intended* meanings and their students' *actual* understandings. This learning is a construction of shared meanings through face-to-face communication and is the core of what teachers and students bring to the classroom. As Barnes (1976) pointed out, classroom communication as a system "is a matter not only of how the teacher sets up classroom relationships and discourse but also of how the pupils interpret what the teacher does" (p. 33). Thus, classroom communication is examined not only in terms of what actually occurs in the classroom, but also in terms of what teachers and students *bring* to the classroom—and how that shapes what occurs there. When I say *bring,* I mean the background belief systems of both the teachers and the students.

Students must be able to perceive and respond to what their teachers say and do in class. How are students to respond to teachers? This and other similar questions will be discussed in later chapters of this book. However, it is the teachers who must take most of the responsibility for controlling the patterns of communication established in their classrooms. Barnes (1976) suggested that the language a teacher uses performs two functions simultaneously: it carries the message that a teacher wants to communicate and, at the same time, it conveys certain information—who the teacher is, to whom he or she is talking, and what the teacher believes the situation is (i.e., the teacher's frame of reference). The way a teacher organizes patterns of classroom communication depends on

- the teacher's prior experiences as a student,
- the teacher's theories about how a subject should be learned, and
- the teacher's beliefs about how a subject should be taught.

Students also have a certain responsibility to contribute to and become actively involved in the learning process. As Barnes (1976) suggested, "learning is not just a matter of sitting there waiting to be taught" (p. 18). Students interpret (through their frame of reference) what teachers present them with in class. For example, a teacher might say something during a class that triggers a thought or reaction to something that a student learned five years ago, and this in turn may lead to the student realizing something completely different than what the teacher had intended for a particular lesson. That is why we say there is no one-to-one correspondence between what the teacher teaches and what the students learn from that particular lesson (Cazden, 1988). Again, as Barnes (1976) suggested, every student will "go away with a version of the lesson which in some respects is different from all other pupils' versions, because what each student brings to the lesson will be different" (p. 21). So even though classroom communication may seem haphazard, the works of Mehan (1979) and Barnes (1976) suggest that it is highly regulated and ritualized and that it has patterns that can be identi-fied. Consequently, the framework outlined in this book offers a means for teachers to reflect on the communication and interac-tional patterns that currently exist in their classrooms so that they can consider their expectations about appropriate communication in their classrooms in order to provide optimum learning opportu-nities for their students.

STUDYING COMMUNICATION PATTERNS

Richards and Lockhart (1994) suggested that teachers are often unaware of what they do when they teach and of how their teaching influences learning. This is because teachers are not familiar with the communication patterns that exist in their classes and do not know how to investigate them. However, teachers can reflect on their teaching so that they can understand what is happening in their class-room, and this form of self-inquiry "can reveal important informa-tion about one's teaching" (p. 3).

Consider a study by Duff (2002), who examined the communica-tions in a high school classroom composed of Mandarin/Cantonese-speaking students, Korean-speaking students, and local Canadian English-speaking students and looked at oral communication and social interaction in learning. The study revealed some contradictions and tensions in classroom communication as the teacher tried to understand the Asian cultural identity and the Asian students' class participation with the local English-speaking Canadian students. Even the students' seating arrangements reflected their racial origins, and the English-speaking Canadian students tended to dominate the whole-class discussions even when the topic was about Asian culture. Reasons for this included the Asian students' lack of confidence and comfort in using English and the fear of being wrong. However, on paper tests, the Asian students scored better than the Canadian students. Interviews with the students indicated that some Asian students felt no need to speak up, while others felt intimidated by the locals. The teacher had no realization of problems in her classes except that "the Asian students were not participating" and did not go beyond this realization. It was only after interacting with the researcher that the teacher tried to consciously change the communi-cation patterns in her classes.

It is important for teachers to study the communication patterns they have set up in their classrooms because in doing so, they can attempt to seek answers to the following questions (adapted from Barnes, 1976):

- How are patterns of communication set up in class?
- Who has decided these patterns of talk?
- What are the effects of these patterns of talk on student participation?
- How do these patterns change?
- How do the students (and teachers) learn them?
- How much of this communication contributes to student learning, and how much performs other functions (what are these functions)?
- Does the teacher's behavior match his or her stated intentions and beliefs?

It is equally important for the students to understand these established patterns of classroom communications so that they will be able to understand what the teacher expects from them. In fact, students must be able to *read* what the teachers want from them because this is rarely stated directly by teachers; student must be able to read *what, why, when,* and *how* they are expected to communicate in the classroom (Mehan, 1979). Students need to have gained *classroom communicative competence* (explored in Chapter 2) in both the social and the interactional requirements in order to be successful learners in the classroom. Even though research tells us that classroom communications between the teacher and students seem to follow a set formula and many teachers tend to rigidly control it, it should be noted that this book takes the stance that day-to-day classroom communications are actively negotiated between teachers and students and that this daily need to negotiate and renegotiate has an impact on learning. As Barnes (1976) stated: "Classroom learning can be best seen as an interaction between the teacher's meanings, and those of his [or her] pupils, so that what they take away is partly shared and partly unique to each of them" (p. 22).

REFLECTING ON CLASSROOM COMMUNICATION

A classroom is a unique context because it is the only context in which communication structures exist where one person (the teacher) is responsible for establishing the speech event from beginning to end. In a classroom, the teacher, because of his or her unique status, is the sole person responsible for what is said, who says it, and what is to be said (generally speaking). The teacher is responsible for (but may not be successful in) ensuring that the communications are clear and smooth and that the other people in the room (the students) understand these communications and are aware of what is expected of them. It is hoped that by reading and reflecting on the contents of this book, teachers will become more aware of the patterns that currently exist in their classrooms and will be able to evaluate whether these patterns provide opportunities for their students to learn. If they discover that this is not the case, then they may take steps to change the communication patterns so that their students can optimize their learning.

CHAPTER TWO

I Treat Them All the Same

Exploring Classroom Communicative Competence

I still remember the day, almost 20 years ago, when I saw the provocative title "I Treat Them All the Same" (Biggs & Edwards, 1991). It prompted me to ask myself: "Do I treat them all the same?" It was the first time I really looked at *all* my students and examined how I set up communications in my classes. Until then, I took everything for granted and assumed that *all* my students fully understood what was required of them during particular activities and in my classroom. I had a sudden realization that I may have been unwittingly blocking opportunities for my students to learn with the communication patterns I had established in my classroom.

In this chapter, I will first describe the seminal study reported by Biggs and Edwards (1991) to serve as a backdrop for a discussion of classroom communicative and interactional competence. The chapter then outlines what can happen when the language of the home is different from the language of the classroom (which, for purposes of this book, I am assuming is Standard English) and when the corresponding communication patterns of the home language are different from the established communication patterns in the classroom.

"I Treat Them All the Same"

The Biggs and Edwards (1991) study took place in England and examined the interactions of five teachers (all white, majority teachers) working within multiethnic classes (of mostly Panjabi children, the largest minority group). Specifically, the researchers were interested in looking into the underachievement of ethnic minority children (EMC) by trying to identify patterns of language behavior that may have placed them at some disadvantage and that could be mediated through language. Generally, they discovered that all five teachers interacted more frequently with white children than with the EMC in the following categories:

- Interaction
- Exchanges lasting more than 30 seconds
- Discussion on a particular task
- Extended exchanges

Biggs and Edwards (1991) discovered that the EMC adopted a topic-associating-style approach to classroom communication, while the white children adopted a topic-centered style. The teachers found it easier to relate to the white children because they could expand classroom communications directly through the comments and questions that they used in everyday speech, be it in the classroom or in their homes. However, the same teachers could not understand how the EMC children communicated. This misunderstanding could have stemmed from the fact that these children all came from a cultural background that included informal or experiential learning, usually characterized by little direct verbal interaction, in which skills tended to be acquired through observation and imitation and where immediate verbal feedback (including evaluation and criticism) was rare. In addition, there was little pressure for systematic testing at various stages in the learning process within their cultural backgrounds. However, when placed in the English school system, the students were faced with a classroom communication style that included more direct verbal instruction in which skills tended to be acquired through drill and practice, rather than observation and imitation, and where there was a greater emphasis placed on giving feedback to the students and checking directly for understanding (tests).

Biggs and Edwards (1991) also found that the teachers tended to discriminate in terms of gender. They initiated fewer interactions with all girls, whatever their cultural background: girls were given fewer directions, were reprimanded less than boys, and took up less teacher time than boys. Yet the teachers were completely unaware that their behavior may have been discriminatory in effect, if not in intent. Of course, the researchers recognized an urgent need to sensitize the teachers to the ways in which they interacted with different groups of students.

It is important to recognize and remediate examples of institutionalized racism so that we can provide equality of opportunity for all children, many of whom come from backgrounds and experiences that are very different from the majority. We must consider that our students' ethnic, cultural, religious, and linguistic backgrounds may be very different from those of the majority in our schools. Consequently, there is an important need for teachers to be able to recognize, understand, and reflect on how communication patterns influence (positively or negatively) their students' learning. Teachers should reflect on how patterns of communication are set up in their classes and how these patterns of communication either provide or block opportunities for *all* students to learn—regardless of their gender or cultural, ethnic, linguistic, or religious backgrounds. That said, it is equally important for the students to be able to recognize some of these patterns of classroom communications so that they are able to understand what the teacher expects from them. For this, they will have to possess classroom communicative competence.

WHAT IS CLASSROOM COMMUNICATIVE AND INTERACTIONAL COMPETENCE?

Many teachers assume that all the participants in a classroom know how to communicate and interact and that their interactions are mostly smooth. In other words, we teachers assume that all our students have some kind of *classroom communicative and interactional competence*— "knowledge of and competence in the structural, functional, social, and interactional norms that govern classroom communication" (Johnson, 1995, p. 160). That is, teachers assume that students are able to understand classroom etiquette for appropriate interaction in the classroom (Richards & Lockhart, 1994). For example, are the students required to raise their hands and wait to be called on by the teacher before asking or answering a question? Or can they shout out answers and participate more spontaneously? What is the level of formality that operates within the class? Are learners expected, for example, to address the teacher by his or her first name (Tom, Mary) or by a title and last name (Mr. Smith, Dr. Jones)? Other classroom interactional etiquette that students need to know include

- the rules for individual or collaborative work,
- when and how to get assistance or feedback,
- the rules for "display" behavior (when to show their knowledge), and
- when they have the right to challenge the teacher or their peers.

Because the teacher is given responsibility for ensuring that learning takes place in the classroom, it becomes the teacher's responsibility to recognize and adjust instructional practices to the competencies of the students in that classroom. Teachers need to offer supportive learning environments by using appropriate verbal scaffolds in order to make classroom events as predictable as possible for the students so that they can develop communicative competence—so that they know what to expect and what is expected of them in the classroom. For this to happen, Johnson (1995) suggested that teachers must also define classroom communicative competence in terms of what they think their students need to know in order to be able to communicate and interact appropriately in their classes. Unfortunately, not all teachers take the time to evaluate classroom communicative competence and assume that all their students know how to interact.

THINKING ABOUT YOUR OWN CLASSROOM

- Are the students required to raise their hands and wait to be nominated before asking or answering a question, or can they shout out and participate more spontaneously in your classes?
- What level of formality operates within your class?
- How and when are students expected to interact with other students?
- Can students move around the room whenever they want?

- If a student needs help with something, when and how does the student approach you?
- To what extent are your students free to challenge what you say?
- How do you establish that all your students have knowledge of and competence in the structural, functional, social, and interactional norms that govern your classroom communication?
- Observe a class to which you have access. Is the teacher conscious of having set explicit rules for interaction in his or her class? If so, what are these rules? To what extent do the teacher's stated rules match your observations of what actually happened in the classroom?

HOME AND SCHOOL COMMUNICATION DIFFERENCES

Although classroom communication is different than all other types of communication, it usually mirrors a teacher's own communication background—the communication norms and competences that he or she grew up with in the home. In the United States, we can say that the dominant group of teachers is made up of middle-class Americans of European descent (Philips, 1983) and that the way they communicate in their classrooms is similar to how they communicate in their homes, especially in how they ask questions. In fact, according to Powell and Caseau (2004), the dominant communication and interaction pattern in American classrooms is direct and individualistic. However, many of our students come to our classes with communication backgrounds that are different from that of the mainstream educational system or the dominant European background (Johnson, 1995). That difference in the culturally learned ways of communicating can inhibit interaction between teachers and students. Moreover, when our students do not communicate the way we expect them to (i.e., they do not answer questions), then we may mistakenly think they are not intellectually bright. Teachers (especially those who come from the dominant group) must become aware that interaction and communication patterns in the students' homes may be very different from those expected in the school and, as a result, may influence the quantity and quality of the students' learning.

Consider the findings from a study by Susan Philips (1983), who compared the verbal-participation patterns in middle-class mainstream classrooms with the Warm Springs Indian Reservation community in Arizona. She found that the Warm Springs students' willingness to participate was related to the way *verbal interaction* was organized and controlled in the classes. Philips observed that Warm Springs students were less willing to participate verbally in classrooms when asked to speak alone, in front of other students, if called upon by the teacher, or if asked to take any leadership role during a discussion. They were more willing to participate verbally in group activities when there was no distinction between the speaker and the audience and when they could self-select when to speak.

In studying the Warm Springs community, Philips (1983) discovered that learning tasks followed a sequence of extensive listening and watching, followed by supervised participation where older relatives often assisted children with breaking the task into smaller parts so that they could successfully complete it. This was followed by self-initiated self-testing of what was learned. Philips observed that the use of speech in the above activities was *minimal,* with few verbal instructions given, and that competence was demonstrated through completing the task itself. Thus, Philips recognized the striking differences in communication and interaction patterns between the Warm Springs community and other school systems. In fact, the teachers in mainstream communities had a total misconception of the reasons for the Warm Springs children's reluctance to speak in class. They judged the children as incompetent rather than looking at the different communication norms in each community.

Similar results were discovered in other research studies of minority children from communication backgrounds different from the dominant group, such as the Kamehameha Early Education Program (KEEP) study of Polynesian children in Hawaii (Au, 1980) and Heath's (1983) work in rural Appalachia. These studies confirmed that there are ways of talking and interacting in some communities that are not the same as what the dominant culture sees as classroom communicative and interactional competence. The result is that some of our students are unnecessarily stigmatized as inferior learners in our classrooms.

In fact, we can distinguish between cultures that communicate with high-context messages and ones that communicate with low-context messages. For cultures (such as Japanese, Korean, Chinese, and Latino communities) communicating with high-context messages, most of the relevant information is said to be internalized in the person and much of the meaning is implied (Powell & Caseau, 2004). In contrast, Powell and Caseau (2004) suggested that cultures that communicate with low-context messages include a lot of detailed information where "uncertainty is reduced and understandings are obtained through expressed verbal codes" (p. 47). Low-context exchanges are found in many American classrooms where both teachers and students are expected to be clear, direct, and explicit in their communications. Thus, teachers from low-context cultures may find it challenging to accommodate students from high-context cultures.

Thus, teachers should become more informed and enlightened and should take a tolerant rather than an exclusionary stance toward discourse-level differences between the language of the home and the language of the classroom. Teachers should first become aware of the communication patterns that currently exist in their own classrooms by looking at

- classroom communication and interaction structures,
- the speaking rights and obligations of all the participants in the classroom,
- how tasks are sequenced,
- their own questions, and
- their use of nonverbal communication.

The subsequent chapters in this book will provide guidance in undertaking this examination. Teachers can then conduct various action research projects to investigate their students' background cultures, home languages, and the verbal interaction patterns in these home languages to determine if they are different from the norms of the classroom. If there are differences, teachers need to foster respect for the cultural identity of all their students.

THINKING ABOUT YOUR OWN CLASSROOM

- What are the "learned ways of talking" in your classroom?
- Identify students in your classroom whose first language is different from that spoken at school. Are students who come from cultures that are different from the majority culture disadvantaged in any way? How do you know they are or are not?
- What is your understanding of the following idea: when children of different cultural backgrounds come together in a classroom, efforts should be made to allow for diversity by changing the way learning and the measurement of success take place (from Philips, 1972, 1983).

(Continued)

(Continued)

- In Chicano communities in the United States, Mexican-American mothers do not use praise, questions, or negative feedback very often. Instead, they rely on visual cues to attract children's attention. Contrast this to European-American mothers who use praise, ask questions, and rely less on modeling or use of visual cues. Outline the different challenges children from Chicano communities may encounter when trying to communicate in classrooms where the teacher and other students are mostly of European descent.

GENDER DIFFERENTIATION

When we talk about gender, we must distinguish between sex, which is a biological designation, and gender, which is a socially constructed designation. Ivy and Backlund (2000) maintained that the family is the most influential agent of gender socialization and that the attitudes and expectations established in and by the family are carried over into the school arena. As pointed out in the Biggs and Edwards's (1991) study, gender has been an issue in classroom participation for some time now. In the past, teachers had a tendency to call on male rather than female students in their classes. This had an effect on their learning because female students felt less motivated to contribute to the lessons. One study (see Brophy & Good, 1991, for details) suggested that subject matter may affect teachers' treatment of male and female students. In reading, female students may receive more instructional time than male students and thus have a higher percentage of academic contact with teachers. However, the opposite may be true for mathematics, where male students may have more academic contacts with teachers than female students. That said, despite the many studies on the effects of gender on learning style, Powell and Caseau (2004) maintained that there is no overwhelming evidence to conclude that "males are superior in some intellectual endeavors and females are superior in others" (p. 73). The point here is that teachers should become more aware of their attitudes toward the gender issue in their classrooms because, as Powell and Caseau

(2004) pointed out, "a teacher's attitude about gender influences the way he or she manages a classroom and affects his or her expectations about student ability" (p. 69).

THINKING ABOUT YOUR OWN CLASSROOM

Sadker and Sadker (1994) summarized a lot of research on gender differences in classroom communication and made the following points; as you read each point, make a note of what you think of each point and how each point plays out in your classroom:

- Teachers tend to communicate more with boys than with girls in the classroom.
- Teachers tend to ask more complex and abstract questions of boys.
- For class assignments, teachers tend to give more detailed instructions to boys than to girls.
- Teachers tend to praise boys more often than girls for the content of their work, but tend to praise girls more often than boys for the neatness of their work.

COMMUNICATION APPREHENSION

One final aspect of classroom communicative competence concerns students who experience discomfort when communicating in public, irrespective of their ethnic or socioeconomic backgrounds. Students who experience communication apprehension tend to avoid situations in which they must talk in public. Consequently, they may be misunderstood as being uncooperative students and receive lower grades than students who do not have such apprehension. McCroskey and McCroskey (2002) suggested some teaching strategies to help reduce communication apprehension for such challenged students. Teachers can reduce oral communication demands by avoiding testing through talk, grading on participation, and calling on students randomly. The point here is that when students do not communicate the way we think they should, we should be aware that they may be suffering from communication apprehension.

REFLECTING ON CLASSROOM COMMUNICATIVE COMPETENCE

What we teachers think our students should know about how to communicate and interact in our classrooms may be very different from what our students think and know. Much of these differences can be attributed to the language and interactional patterns of the home versus those of the school, as well as to gender socialization and communication apprehension. What teachers can do is explore their own standards for classroom communicative competence and be certain that their classrooms are culture-neutral and gender-safe environments, as well as environments where all students feel included and secure. Teachers should increase their own awareness of these issues so that they can be better prepared to facilitate student learning.

CHAPTER THREE

You Talk Like a Teacher

Collecting and Analyzing Classroom Communication

Has anyone (especially friends who are not teachers) ever said that you "talk like a teacher?" Do you feel the need to initiate conversations with your friends? Do you feel the need to "keep the conversation going" when it lags a bit? Are you uncomfortable with silence in conversations with your friends? Do others think that you tend to control conversations and even evaluate them? Do they think you feel as if you have to provide feedback to them after they respond? Positive responses to these questions are indications that you do talk like a teacher because you are subconsciously using evaluations in conversations with your friends, not to mention expressing a deep need to initiate many of the conversations. Teachers often do not realize that communication that happens naturally outside the classroom is different from what occurs inside the classroom.

Classroom communication has been called a "game" (Belleck, Kliebard, Hyman, & Smith, 1966) in which the teacher, either consciously or unconsciously (the latter is most prevalent), uses language to establish patterns of communication. As Briscoe, Arriaza, and Henze (2009) maintained, the more we learn about language, "the more we notice it in our everyday lives—we begin to hear details and notice patterns we didn't notice before. This noticing can happen in the form of self-monitoring the language of others around us" (p. 36). However, many teachers are not aware of the communication patterns that exist in their classes. This chapter describes the underlying classroom communication structures and then explains how teachers can begin to collect, code, and analyze their own classroom communication so that they can examine the underlying structure in their own classes.

BASIC CLASSROOM COMMUNICATION STRUCTURE

The underlying communication structure inside the classroom is different from what occurs outside the classroom. In most classrooms, the communication structure follows a pattern of

1. the teacher initiates (*I*),

2. a student (or students) responds (*R*), and

3. the teacher evaluates (*E*) the response.

As introduced in Chapter 1, Mehan (1979) referred to this as *IRE*. The following example illustrates this underlying communication structure.

Basic Classroom Communication Structure

1: Teacher: What day is today?   (*Initiation*)

2: Students: Monday.   (*Response*)

3: Teacher: Very good. Monday.   (*Evaluation*)

In Turn 1, the teacher asks the students what day it is. The students respond in Turn 2 that it is Monday. The teacher evaluates the response in Turn 3 by saying the answer is correct and then repeats the students' earlier correct response. This brief exchange shows how a teacher uses language to manage and control classroom communication (Johnson, 1995).

However, outside classrooms, it is unusual to find participants in everyday conversations evaluating responses to solicits; rather, participants usually acknowledge such solicits. For example, using the same examples in Turns 1 and 2, in this conversation Turn 3 is an acknowledgment:

Communication Structure Outside Classroom

1: Person 1:   What day is today?   (*Initiation*)

2: Person 2:   Monday.   (*Response*)

3: Person 1:   Thank you.   (*Acknowledgment*)

We can say that the underlying structure of classroom communication distinguishes itself from other forms of communication in that teachers usually respond to what their students say not by replying to it or acknowledging it, but by evaluating it. In fact, the research by Belleck et al. (1966) revealed that nearly one-third of teacher communications consisted of evaluating their students' responses and that many teachers were unaware of this. If a teacher's classroom communication continually follows the teacher initiated *IRE* structure, it can be problematic. If teachers constantly evaluate their students' responses, the students may interpret these evaluations as devaluing their opinions—especially if these evaluations have been negative—and in the worst case, as an attempt to silence them from contributing opinions of their own. This undermines the students' ability to contribute successfully to the lesson (Barnes, 1976). Classroom communication must allow for variability in the underlying communication structures if lessons are to be effective (Mehan, 1979).

VARIABILITY IN CLASSROOM COMMUNICATION STRUCTURE

Variability in classroom communication, called marked (unusual) patterns, can take many forms, such as student initiations and teacher responses followed by student evaluations or students performing all three *IRE* moves (Mehan, 1979). This is illustrated in the following transcript I prepared and coded of student-initiated variability in the classroom communication structure in an English language class where third-grade students were encouraged to initiate and "take the floor" (the teacher's words) whenever they wanted to. The teacher's stated objectives in this phonics lesson were that the students would be able to recognize and read *nd, ng,* and *nk* in words. The transcript occurs midway through the lesson and outlines an exchange where certain students became curious about the meaning of the words they were pronouncing and one of them (Jimmy) noticed that he had heard a word before on TV.

Student Initiation: Turns 1–12

1: Jimmy: What is a plank? I heard it on TV. (*I, student initiated*)

2: Teacher: What is a plank? This is a plank, a wooden plank [*shows a photo*]. (*R*)

3: Sean: I see this before. My father used something like this before. (*R*)

4: Teacher: He used it for what? (*I*)

5: Sean: To fix something. (*R*)

6: Teacher: To fix something . . . some people cut the wooden thing into smaller pieces and maybe they make something. (*R*)

7: Sean: They put on my . . . (*R*)

8: Teacher: You see the bookshelf behind? OK, you see the bookshelf where you put your water bottles? (*I*)

9: Sean: Um hmm. (*R*)

10: Teacher: What is that made of? (*I*)

11: Sean: Planks. (*R*)

12: Teacher: Planks. Wooden planks. That's right. (*E*)

This exchange clearly shows that during this phase of the lesson, the students took control of communications by choosing the topic for discussion (in this case, their curiosity about the meaning of the word *plank* that Jimmy had heard before) and initiating the first question after they all had spent time pronouncing it (Turn 1). Then, the teacher took up Jimmy's initiation by responding to his query (Turn 2), which was followed by a response from another student, Sean (Turn 3). The remainder of the exchange was then between Sean and the teacher, and it followed the traditional *IRE* sequence. We must wonder about the teacher's comfort level with the opening turns where the students led the exchange; some teachers may be uncomfortable with such an exchange because of the perception that they may be losing control of the class with students speaking "out of turn." However, even though the students initiated and the teacher responded in the above example, it does not mean that the teacher had lost control of her classroom communications. Rather, the teacher had full control of the communication in her class, and she was very comfortable with her students taking control of classroom topics. After class, she mentioned that she always hopes that her students are "engaged in constructive discussions that are meaning-focused." Consequently, the students in this class can feel that their teacher values their input, and as a result, they are not afraid to initiate communication during the class, thus taking responsibility for their own learning.

How to Examine Classroom Communication Patterns

In order to understand how our underlying classroom communication patterns either set up or block opportunities for our students' learning, we teachers need to investigate and reflect on the communication patterns in our own classrooms. We must gather concrete data about the communications that exist in our classrooms and then use the information from the data to make informed decisions about our teaching. Throughout this chapter, I will be calling the model of collecting and analyzing classroom communication data *record-transcribe-analyze.*

Collecting Classroom Communication Data

The most important type of concrete classroom communication data a teacher should collect is a recording of the communications and a record of this recording in the form of a written classroom transcript. If we rely on our memory of classroom communications and events, we may miss some important data because we all have selective memories. I cannot begin to tell you how many times I have said to other teachers about my own recordings and transcriptions: "I never realized that I . . . ." You can fill in the blank with whatever realization you can imagine because I have had all of them, from ". . . asked so many questions," to ". . . talked for 95% of the class time," and so on. Recordings and transcriptions are the best concrete evidence we teachers can get about our work.

We can collect this type of concrete data by placing an audio recorder or video recorder in our classroom. I have found that two recorders are probably necessary: one near the teacher to pick up what he or she is saying, and the other in the middle of the classroom to record what students are saying. If students break up for group or pair work, place the audio recorder in the middle of one of the groups because it may be impossible to record what each group is saying.

THINKING ABOUT YOUR OWN CLASSROOM

Audio- or videorecord your class. Now play the recording and try to answer the following questions:

- What did you notice first about the recording?
- Did you focus on your voice (and physical appearance if you used video)?
- Did you notice your pronunciation?
- What did you notice about your students?
- Are you comfortable with the speed at which you heard yourself speak?
- If your students did not respond, what did you do?
- How much wait-time did you allow in which your students could think before answering your questions?
- How did you check on your students' understanding?
- What kind of reinforcement did you give and how often?

Transcribing the Recording

Once the classroom communication data has been collected, the teacher then needs to transcribe the recording; this can be the most painful part of the whole process because it can take a long time to transcribe a one-hour class. Keep the transcript as simple as possible by naming each participant and then numbering each move (when someone speaks a turn), and keep to the original wording as accurately as possible (do not change it to make it more readable). It may not be necessary to transcribe the entire recording; teachers can decide what aspect of the classroom communications they are interested in knowing more about. Fanselow (1987) suggested that transcriptions be made at certain intervals or at special events that the teacher wants to investigate. For example, teachers may only be interested in reflecting on the impact of their verbal instructions in their classes, so all they need to do is listen to and transcribe those parts of the tape that show the teacher giving instructions and then the turns immediately after this (for about five minutes) to see what impact these instructions have had on their students' learning. Other topics could include the type and frequency of teacher (and student) questions, how tasks are set up in their classes, or the type of language in use in group discussions (if teachers of English language learners wish to focus on this aspect of classroom communication). As noted, transcribing takes a lot of time; some have said it takes six to eight minutes to transcribe *one minute* of recording. It may not be feasible to transcribe the whole lesson. If it is not, I suggest the following alternative after you have recorded the lesson:

1. Play it through once, making a record of the time at which each *new episode or activity begins.*

2. Write down a phrase to summarize what happens in each episode.

3. Select episodes that seem likely to provide the evidence relevant to the question in focus.

4. Only transcribe that portion of the tape.

That said, I would suggest that each teacher try to transcribe a full class recording at least once during his or her career. One way to do this is to ask your school to provide funding for you to hire a transcriber to help you.

Analyzing Classroom Communication

After transcribing classroom communication, the teacher can analyze and interpret the data. Many different methodological frameworks have been developed for analyzing and interpreting classroom discourse (see, for example, Belleck et al., 1966; Flanders, 1970; Sinclair & Coulthard, 1975). The method for analyzing classroom communication that I prefer is the one devised by Hugh Mehan (1979) for his ethnographic work—specifically his suggestion of the *IRE* structured pattern of classroom communication. This *IRE* pattern has been used by educational researchers as the most typical pattern of classroom communication. This pattern has been criticized because it restricts the role students play in the construction of knowledge since the teacher makes most of the initiations and evaluates most of the student responses. This in turn restricts classroom talk to "final draft" teacher talk rather than more exploratory talk in which students' prior and current beliefs are considered and knowledge is coconstructed. Mehan also included nonverbal behaviors in his method because they can provide cues both to discourse structure and to the interpretation of individual utterances.

After making interpretations about the communications that exist in their classes, teachers can decide if they want to make any variations in the patterns that they have discovered. In this way, teachers can take more responsibility for the decisions they make about their classes. Teachers can also share the transcribed data with their colleagues and even their students. A group of teachers can record one class, transcribe the communication, and share the transcription with each other, thus providing examples of authentic and live interaction that all can learn from. In this way colleagues can, depending on the purpose of the reflections, further analyze transcripts for style of interaction, turn taking, questioning, and the various communication strategies used. When sharing this with their students, depending on their level, teachers can simplify, reduce, or omit some of the communication if it seems overwhelming. When teachers share their transcripts and analyze these classroom communications with their students, there is a good chance that these same students may be more successful in their communications inside and outside of the classroom.

When teachers review transcripts that are coded in the *IRE* system, they are likely to discover that students produce different speech patterns in response to different tasks, and as a result, the teachers will also have to adjust their own particular speech patterns. Given that teachers use communicative tasks to evaluate students' abilities, a better understanding of the influence of specific activities on learner discourse will likely lead teachers to use a greater variety of tasks in order to gain a more comprehensive picture of their students' abilities. By *recording, transcribing,* and *analyzing* our communications, and at times our students' communications, we teachers can gain useful insight into the effect of our instructional tasks on our students' development in our classes.

As was discussed in Chapter 2, a *record-transcribe-analyze* mode of teacher reflection may also shed some light on the linguistic patterns of students from different cultural backgrounds—especially when the language of the home is different from the language of the school, which calls for a different knowledge of classroom communicative competence. For example, some students may engage in "overlap" while the teacher is speaking or while another student is talking. Rather than berating our students for being disruptive, we may want to consider that they may have a different level of classroom communicative and interactional competence. For some linguistic groups, this discourse behavior can be interpreted as a signal of engagement and involvement; however, other speakers may view it as an interruption and imposition on their speaking rights.

These discrepancies will appear in the *IRE* coded classroom communication transcript. Thus, teachers can use the *record-transcribe-analyze* technique outlined in this chapter to study cross-cultural interactions in their classrooms, further helping students identify different communication strategies and recognize their potential for miscommunication so that *all* our students can have an enriching experience in our classroom.

THINKING ABOUT YOUR OWN CLASSROOM

Using the transcript (or part of the transcript) you have prepared from a lesson, analyze your classroom communications:

- First code the transcript with the *IRE* coding system.
- What is the underlying communication structure in your class as a result of the *IRE* coding?
- Do you notice any variations from the usual teacher controlled *IRE* sequence?
- Did you find any places where your students were initiating? If so, did you notice many evaluations (or none) by you the teacher or the other students?
- What percentage of the time were you talking, and what percentage were your students talking? Are you comfortable with the results?
- What percentage of the time was your speech in the form of a question? To what percentage of your questions did you already know the answers?
- What other classroom communication features are you now aware of in your classroom?

REFLECTING ON CLASSROOM COMMUNICATION DATA

Hurt, Scott, and McCrosky (1978) remarked that communication in the classroom is the difference between *knowing* and *teaching,* and this emphasizes the central role of communication for successful instruction. Knowledge about classroom communication patterns can help teachers make more informed decisions about teaching so that all students can experience a truly effective learning environment. Teachers can gain this knowledge by capturing the oral communications that occur in their classrooms, and the only valuable way of accomplishing this is to audio- or videorecord (with audio) the class and then to transcribe what was said to produce a lesson transcript. Next, teachers can code and analyze the lesson transcript in order to look for patterns that emerge and to decide if the communication that is happening leads to maximum learning in that classroom. Of course, reviewing audio and video recordings can add to this knowledge by revealing the prosodic features of the teacher's voice, such as stress and intonation, which are not visible in a transcript—not to mention all the nonverbal information provided by facial expressions and body language. Chapter 8 covers this aspect of classroom communication in more detail.

CHAPTER FOUR

Why Don't They Do What I Ask?

Developing Effective Classroom Participation

M any times we teachers come out of our classes wondering why our students did not respond the way we had anticipated and hoped they would. We may blame them for not responding, yet we could be at fault if we did not give clear instructions about what we wanted the students to accomplish during a lesson. We must remember that it is the teacher who is responsible for making sure that the learning tasks he or she sets up are clear to all involved and that the participants are aware of what is expected of them. This chapter explores how teachers can use language effectively to set academic learning tasks and ensure that students clearly perceive what social participation is expected from them during these tasks.

A BAD BEGINNING

Have you ever started a class and noticed immediately that your students seemed to be in a different world? They do not get what you want to teach them at that particular moment even though you are fired up and ready to go, nor do they want to move on from an issue you have already covered and know you are finished with. It could be either that you were not clear enough in your opening verbal instructions or that your nonverbal expressions did not match your verbal instructions (see Chapter 8 for more details on nonverbal communication).

The following example from an elementary school ESL (English as a Second Language) class on reading comprehension, in which a teacher is attempting to begin her class, shows exactly what can happen in a busy classroom when the teacher has one objective but the students have another (adapted from Tsui, 1995). Below are the opening 26 turns of the class, which lasts no more than three minutes. The students had just sat in their seats when some of them spoke loudly to the teacher:

1: Students: Do we need to draw a picture?

2: Teacher: Draw what picture?

3: Students: *[Overlapping talk]*

4: Teacher: No, you don't have to draw the pictures, just write the sentences. All right, now will you take out your Green Book Four?

5: Students: Mrs. K, do we need to write number one on the book?

6: Teacher: No, you don't have to write number one, otherwise it would be twelve pairs of sentences, wouldn't it? Eleven pairs.

7: Students: Do we get the Green Book Four?

8: Teacher: Green Book Four, yes. You know it's a reading lesson, why don't you get it out ready? All right, now, Green Book Four. Last week, we were reading about Lalloon Land. Where is Lalloon Land supposed to be?

9: Students: *[Silence]*

10: Teacher: Do you think there is a real country called Lalloon Land?

11: Students: No.

12: Teacher: No. But in the story, what does it say about Lalloon Land?

13: Students: *[Silence]*

14: Teacher: Have you been to Lalloon Land?

15: Students: *[Shake heads]*

16: Student: *[Raises hand]*

17: Teacher: Michele?

18: Michele: Can we give in our grammar on um Wednesday?

19: Teacher: Can you give in your grammar on Wednesday? You have a lot of homework for tomorrow?

20: Michele: Yes, yes.

21: Students: We have our last exercise.

22: Teacher: You have to do . . .

23: Students: Our last exercise.

24: Teacher: Oh that's because you have been lazy and didn't do your work properly. Right?

25: Students: No.

26: Teacher: So I'm sorry, you have to do it, otherwise I won't be able to finish marking your books to give you back before the holidays.

In the previous chapter, I said that transcripts can provide concrete evidence of what actually happens in our classroom rather than what we think happens. By analyzing our transcripts, we can tell if our class is going according to our plans and our instructional objectives. With a transcript, we can move beyond feelings about our classes and intuitions about what should happen; the transcript tells us exactly what has happened. This teacher was very surprised at what she discovered when she saw this transcript (although we do not know if she noticed that she may have made an inappropriate comment in Turn 24); it is really amazing what just 26 opening turns of a classroom communication transcript can tell us about the direction of a class.

This exchange reveals many facts about communication patterns that exist in that classroom. From the opening turns we can clearly see and realize that the lesson is not proceeding according to the teacher's plan—we have all been there before, wanting to get started on a lesson or topic and getting a little frustrated when our students are not coming along with us as quickly as we would like. Can you feel or sense the teacher's frustration level growing as the class progresses? For example, if we look at Turns 1 to 4 in the example above, we can see that the teacher is trying to get to her main pedagogical objective—to teach reading from a prescribed text (the "Green Book Four")—and assumes the students are all following her until we get to Turn 16 where Michele raises her hand to ask a question about something completely different. Your first impression at this turn may have been that Michele was going to answer the question the teacher asked in Turn 14, as was my first impression; however, we can see from Michele's response in Turn 18 that she and the other students had some anxieties about their homework, and thus, they were not following the academic task that the teacher was trying to set and probably would not do so unless and until the teacher addressed their anxieties.

We can clearly see that the students in this class had a different agenda and that the teacher was not able to pick up on this until near the end of the opening turns. In fact, the teacher's frame of reference and the students' frame of reference were completely different from the very start of the class: The teacher wanted to get on with the lesson and start teaching the reading passage from the text, but the students were really worried about their homework assignment—possibly they did not understand it—and these differences in the frames of reference between the teacher and the students caused interference in the social participation structure of the lesson until the students' anxieties were put to rest. Thus, we teachers must be able to read our students' anxieties and resistances and try to figure out why they may not be tuned into the academic task we are trying to set. If the academic task is not clearly set, this can have a knock-out effect on how the students interact during that lesson or activity with the end result of possible nonparticipation during the lesson.

THINKING ABOUT YOUR OWN CLASSROOM

- Have you ever started a class and immediately noticed that your students seemed to be in a different world? Explain the circumstances of that class and try to remember exactly what happened.
- How do you plan to monitor how you set learning tasks in the future?

ORGANIZING EFFECTIVE CLASSROOM PARTICIPATION

Effective classroom participation will mean different things to different teachers and administrators. For example, if we view our students as having no knowledge of a topic, then we may set up communication in our classroom where students listen and the teacher talks as an expert. This follows a *transmission model* of communication, where the teacher controls what is communicated, who can speak, when, and what they should say. On the other hand, if we think our students posses some prior knowledge, experience, or even beliefs about a particular subject matter, and that they will form (or are capable of forming) their own understanding of what the teacher introduces, this is a *constructivist model* of communication. It may be defined as a belief that "learners construct their own meaning from interaction with texts, problems, materials, students, teachers, and other features of the learning environment" (Powell & Caseau, 2004, p. 8). I do not want to say which model a teacher should follow, for it will depend on the lesson objective; rather, the point is that teachers should be aware of how they set up *academic tasks* and how it impacts the *social participation* structure of their lessons in ways that are clearly perceptible to each student in that classroom. However, I do agree with Powell and Caseau (2004) who said that "the relationship between learning and language is at the core of constructivist approaches to education" (p. 8).

Philips (1972) suggested that for students to be able to understand how to participate in a classroom, they have to have the knowledge of classroom procedures about who can talk and when during class. If our students are able to understand what is expected from them in a lesson and from a particular activity, then there is a good chance that they may learn what we intend for them to learn. In order to recognize what is expected of them, they must understand how the teacher structures classroom communication in that lesson. Erickson (1982) maintained that teachers were responsible for setting two main interrelated structures that influence student participation—the academic task structure and the social participation structure. The *academic task structure* details how subject matter is to be sequenced in a lesson, and the *social participation structure* outlines who can speak, to whom, and about what, and it includes turn taking.

Setting the Academic Task Structure

The best way to talk about setting academic tasks is to use a transcript example from a real class for the remainder of this chapter as a backdrop for our discussion. This transcript outlines how teachers can use different techniques when setting academic tasks in their classes and how these affect the social participation structure of the class. The class example is a vocabulary lesson from an elementary school (Grade 6). The first part of the lesson is conducted in an open field near the school because the teacher wants to use the natural environment and cue cards to aid the students in their understanding of the different components of a tree. The teacher's stated lesson objective is that the students should be able to name the different parts of a tree as a follow-up lesson to a previous one on plants.

According to Mehan (1979), most classroom communications have three main phases: *opening, instructional,* and *closing.* Usually the teacher sets the main academic task during the opening phase, where specific information about the academic task and how it is to be accomplished is exchanged between the teacher and the students.

Lesson Opening

Turns 15–17

15: Teacher: OK, we saw the cactus last week and what else, John?

16: John: Hibiscus.

17: Teacher: Hibiscus, very good!

Turns 21–23

21: Teacher: Plant, OK, flower. Now what do we learn about flowers?

What is that thing called? Remember your sunflower that went "flop"? So what is that thing called?

22: Students: Flower. Petal. Stalk.

23: Teacher: Stalk. Good!

Turn 32

32: Teacher: Petals, good. John. OK, today we are going to focus on trees. OK, tell me the difference between the tree and the plant, the flower.

In this opening phase, the teacher begins setting the academic task by first reviewing (Turns 15 to 17 and Turns 21 to 23) the concepts and terms introduced in an earlier lesson to ensure that the students have developed a joint understanding for further teaching. Then in Turn 32, the academic task is established by the teacher as she introduces the topic for the day's lesson. In addition, when the teacher wants to move from one part of an academic task to another, she uses the technique of *back referencing* (Edwards & Mercer, 1989) to ensure a smooth transition from one part to another as sequenced in the academic task structure indicated in Turns 230 to 232 from the same lesson:

Turns 230–232

230: Teacher: Just now, we have seen how a tree looked right? We are going through the different parts of a tree. Last week, we did it on a flower and you made . . . some of you made beautiful sunflowers as well, right? No?

231: Students: Yes!

232: Teacher: Now today, I am going to give you this picture. Some of you will receive . . .

However, sometimes after the academic task has been set, a lesson derailment (Allwright & Bailey, 1991) of the academic task structure can occur that makes it very difficult for the teacher to return to the academic task he or she has set. This can be seen in Turns 35 to 43, where the teacher has to stop her teaching because Jerry is standing up instead of sitting.

Turns 35–43

35: Teacher: Why are you standing up?

36: Jerry: I cannot see.

37: Teacher: Sit. Jerry.

38: Teacher: Cactus.

39: Jerry: OK, sit.

40: Teacher: Sit.

41: Jerry: OK. Sit. My legs hurt.

42: Teacher: If you don't sit, you go over to that side. I mean it!

43: Teacher: OK, we saw the cactus. . . .

In Turn 43, the teacher uses the term *OK* to signal the eventual return to the academic task structure after a repair has been made.

Establishing the Social Participation Structure

The social participation structure refers to the allocation of the interactional rights and obligations of participants that shape classroom communications (Johnson, 1995). In many classrooms, teachers usually call on students to answer a question, and once a student is selected, that student is obligated to make a response and speak until the turn is complete. In Turn 120, which follows, the teacher directs another initiation to the same student without stating the student's name directly. The student understands that it is still her turn to speak and completes her turn. In this way, the pattern of teacher initiating, student responding, and teacher evaluating or asking another question is established:

Turns 118–121

118: Teacher: Right, Mary? What is this called?

119: Mary: Twig.

120: Teacher: Show me a twig.

121: Mary: There *[points to a twig]*.

TEACHER TALK

In most classrooms, the teacher is seen as the main player in the classroom in creating the type of talk he or she wants to encourage, and this will, more often than not, depend on the pedagogical objectives of each lesson. Teachers may not realize that two types of teacher talk are present in many classrooms—*exploratory talk* and *final draft talk* (Barnes, 1976). When teachers use exploratory talk, they are admitting that they may not know all the answers or have the final word on an issue. A type of tentativeness characterizes exploratory talk, where teachers may be seen to be rearranging their own thoughts as they speak. Exploratory talk is characterized by a teacher's use of hedges and qualifiers, tag questions, and some disclaimers. Hedges and qualifiers such as *possibly* and *I would think so* take away from the certainty of what the teacher is saying. Similarly, vocal fillers and hesitations such as *um, uh, you know,* and *like* are also examples of teacher talk that indicates that the teacher has not finalized his or her conclusions. Tag questions take away from the certainty of a teacher's response, as in the following example:

A: Teacher: This chapter is difficult.

B: Teacher: This chapter is difficult, isn't it?

Statement A is a statement of fact by the teacher, while statement B is more tentative and allows for the students to agree or disagree. This type of exploratory talk (Statement B) is more inclusive because it invites students into the dialogue. Thus, teachers do not use a type of language that emphasizes their authority as the expert on the topic at hand, which is characteristic of final draft talk.

Final draft talk, as in Statement A, indicates that the teacher has the last word and, in contrast to exploratory talk, does not invite students to dialogue with the teacher. Barnes (1976) maintained, "Final draft language is the contrary of exploratory" (p. 108). Whereas exploratory speech is represented by some conversational detours where the teacher is hesitant to give a definite answer or evaluation, final draft talk is a more polished exchange in which the teacher follows a direct *IRE* sequence: the teacher initiates, the students respond, and the teacher evaluates. This suggests that when a teacher uses a lot of final draft talk in his or her lessons, it can adversely affect his or her students' willingness to contribute to a lesson because the teacher is demonstrating that he or she has all the answers. I suggest that many teachers use both final draft and exploratory talk in class but are neither aware of the percentage of the usage of each one nor are aware of the effect of each type.

The following excerpt is a typical example of the type of talk many teachers use in their classes. The transcript is taken from a third grade class on English writing. At the end of the lesson, the teacher wants the students to be able to list the five methods of writing an introduction to a composition and apply one of the five methods to write an introduction for a given piece of writing.

Turns 1–9

1: Teacher: Why do you say it's the past tense?

2: Students: It's better.

3: Teacher: It's better you, eh . . . past tense, right? Because it tells us something in the past. What about punctuation marks?

5: Brian: Include commas.

6: Teacher: Yes, you have to include a comma, and you should be careful in the sense that you have to place all your punctuation marks correctly at the right place. OK? So you have to be very careful in your punctuation so that you will not make eh . . . punctuation mistakes.

7: Teacher: We have *Dialogue*; we have *Flashback*; *What, Where, and When*. We have *Description of Surroundings*. The last one?

8: Larry: About weather. Sunny . . .

9: Teacher: About weather. That is *Description of Surroundings* already. OK, one more. Last one? Think.

This classroom talk was mostly final draft talk. What the students said and how it was said was actually a final presentation for the teacher's approval (Barnes, 1976). That said, there were some instances of exploratory talk too, as in Turn 3, when the teacher is thrown a bit by the students' answer in Turn 2 and shows that she is not entirely clear about how to respond. Turn 6 is also an example of a teacher thinking on her feet and showing us that she may not have all the answers.

THINKING ABOUT YOUR OWN CLASSROOM

- What are the advantages and disadvantages of using final draft talk? Exploratory talk? Which are you more comfortable using in your classes?
- Do you agree with Barnes (1976) who suggested that a teacher should use more exploratory type talk with lots of hesitations, or do you think students may misinterpret this type of talk as evidence that the teacher does not know the answer?

- Do you agree that final draft talk tends to devalue students' opinions?
- Now look at the transcript of your classroom communication and see if you can identify the academic task structure and the social participation structure in your lesson. Try to answer the following questions:

  o When and how did you set up the academic task structure?
  o Which turn(s) is this evident in?
  o Did you plan this, or did it just happen?
  o Did your class generally go according to your plan as evident in the transcript?
  o Was the academic task clear to your students, as evident in the transcript?
  o Which turns tell you this?
  o Did the social participation of the lesson go according to your plans?
  o Were there any lesson derailments that required you to stop teaching and take care of classroom discipline?
  o Which turns tell you this?

Reflecting on Effective Classroom Participation

This chapter suggests that if the teacher consciously uses clear communications (verbal and nonverbal) when setting learning tasks, then the corresponding social participation structure will be clear and the lesson may progress as planned. When classes do not go according to our plan from the very beginning, rather than blaming the students for not being able to follow our lessons, we should look at our own teaching and the way we set our academic tasks. In addition, it also suggests that during the execution of these academic learning tasks, teachers should be aware of their talk and whether it is mostly of the final draft type or the exploratory talk type. I hope you have seen both the need for and the power of classroom communication transcripts and the value of the time it has taken you to transcribe all or part of your classroom communication.

CHAPTER FIVE

What Is 2 + 2?

Examining Teachers' Questions

Two of the most common ways in which teachers communicate with their students during class is by asking (and answering) questions and by providing feedback. This chapter will explore the way teachers use questions, while Chapter 6 will examine teacher feedback. Teachers use questioning at the beginning of their classes to establish who controls the interaction, what the topic is for that class, and who is expected to speak. Many teachers also use questions during the course of the class to constantly check their students' understanding of the particular concepts they are teaching at that time. In fact, teachers use questioning as the most frequent means of communication in their classrooms. Forrestal (1990) discovered that almost 60% of the total time a teacher talks in class involves the use of questioning of some sort, and most of the questions teachers ask their students are those to which the teacher already knows the answers (sometimes called *display-type questions*, such as in the title of this chapter—of course, the answer is 4).

If asked, most teachers have no idea how many questions they ask in each class or what type of questions they favor in their classes. This is problematic because unless teachers become more aware of how and why they use questioning during their classes, this strategy is unlikely to be an effective aid to instruction. This chapter explores the different types and functions of teachers' questions and also addresses an important aspect of questioning—wait-time, or the time a teacher waits for an answer after asking a question.

INFORMANT QUESTIONING STRATEGIES

Generally, most teachers use questioning as a strategy to control the content of a lesson, depending, of course, on the pedagogical purpose of that lesson. For example, a teacher in an informant role who is teaching new information to his or her students will ask direct, information-seeking questions, while a teacher in a facilitator role may want the students to discuss this information in terms of their prior experiences. Most teachers tend to start in an informant role and may or may not move into a facilitator role as the students become more familiar with the topic. In an informant role, teachers use two different questioning strategies to seek specific answers related to lesson content: *preformulation questions* and *reformulation questions* (Johnson, 1995). They first ask *preformulation questions* to provide a cue to the answer they are seeking, and if the students do not understand the initial question, they usually *reformulate* it to make the question easier for students to understand. These reformulation questions are necessary, especially if students fail to understand a teacher's initiations (i.e., the preformulation questions), because this failure to initially understand the content of the lesson can lead to a breakdown in either the academic task structure or the social participation structure of the lesson, or both. This could occur if the teacher's and students' frames of reference do not coincide. It is therefore important that teachers expose students to the different functions of questions and allow students to familiarize themselves with what is expected of them when particular types of questions are asked. Look at the following example that includes the main title of this chapter and records a novice kindergarten teacher's lesson on adding numbers.

Turns 1–13

1: Teacher: Right. Can anybody tell me what 2 + 2 is? **(Preformulation 1)**

2: Students: *[All silent]*

3: Teacher: Nobody knows?

4: Students:	*[All silent]*	
5: Teacher:	OK, look here, I have one apple and one orange in my hand, how many in total do I have? (**Reformulation 1**)	
6: Students:	More than one.	
7: Teacher:	More than one. Correct, I have two.	
8: Teacher:	How many apples and oranges do I have?	
9: Students:	Two.	
10: Teacher:	Very good, two.	
11: Teacher:	Now, I have two apples in my left hand and two oranges in my right hand, so how many do I have in both hands? (**Reformulation 2**)	
12: Students:	Four.	
13: Teacher:	Yes! Four! Yes, good.	

Here, the teacher used two interactive questioning strategies, preformulation and reformulation, to nudge the students toward the answers she was seeking. For the preformulation strategy, the teacher's question provided some cues to the students as to how it should be have been answered. For example, in Turn 1, the teacher asked a preformulated question: "Can anybody tell me what 2 + 2 is?" However, since no one responded, the teacher simplified the question by reformulating it into two separate questions in Turns 5 and 11: "OK, look here, I have one apple and one orange in my hand, how many in total do I have?" and later, "Now, I have two apples in my left hand and two oranges in my right hand, so how many do I have in both hands?" The students came up with the correct answer in Turn 12, thus showing how effective reformulating questions is for our students.

We know that teachers use general questioning techniques (such as the preformulation and reformulation questions just explained) in their classes, yet many remain unaware of their use of this strategy. Furthermore, many teachers don't realize that this lack of information about the questions they use in their classes and the frequency of their usage may actually have a detrimental effect on their students' learning and scholastic achievement because much of their questioning behavior may in fact be ineffective. For example, we teachers must first realize the frequency of the use of questions as a teaching strategy, and then we must ask ourselves if we are overly dominating the communication time in our classes even though we may not mean to or want to do so. In addition, as was already pointed out, we teachers tend to overuse factual questions (where we already know the answers). Are we aware of our usage and does this type of question help our students learn? Although factual questions help teachers ascertain whether or not students understand the content of the lesson, we must beware of turning the whole class into one giant interrogation session. Thus, it is vitally important that teachers become aware of their questioning behaviors and then analyze the usefulness of these questions in helping the students learn. It is imperative that teachers become more aware of not only the number of questions they ask but also the function of their questions, the sequencing of the questions in the lesson, and how long they wait for an answer.

TYPES OF TEACHER QUESTIONS

I have been using the term *question* without examining its meaning. Although we may all think we know what it means, different educators and teachers have different understandings of what a question is. I will outline three different taxonomies of teacher questions.

In an early attempt to analyze teacher questions, Barnes (1976) distinguished, as follows, between four different types of teachers' questions that he observed in secondary schools in England:

1. *Factual:* The *what* questions.

2. *Reasoning:* The *how* and *why* questions of two types:
   a. *closed* (only one answer possible) and
   b. *open* (a number of different answers possible).

3. *Open:* No reasoning required.

4. *Social:* Students' behavior influenced by means of control or appeal.

From this list, Barnes (1976) discovered that the most popular type of question teachers ask is *closed reasoning*. He discovered that *open reasoning questions* were nearly absent from most classrooms. Barnes suggested that this preference for *closed reasoning questions* showed that teachers saw their roles more as transmitters of knowledge than as the people responsible for getting the students involved in the learning process, as in a constructivist teaching philosophy. Again, we can see the importance of teacher awareness of the type of questions asked in class because they are also an indication of a teacher's teaching and learning philosophy. I wonder if teachers will be pleased or shocked when they become more aware of the type of questions they ask in class and their corresponding teaching/learning philosophy. In other words, do their classroom practices (in this case, the type of questions they ask) correctly reflect their teaching philosophy and beliefs?

Brophy and Good (1991) observed similar patterns of teacher questions in the United States when they talked in terms of *higher-order questions* and *lower cognitive level questions,* although they cautioned against making too much of "thought" questions as opposed to "fact" questions. They maintained that even though higher-order questions tend to elicit higher-order responses from students, it is not always true that thought questions (higher-order questions) are always better than factual questions (lower-order or simpler questions) and that varying combinations of these are needed depending of the lesson objective. Brophy and Good also pointed out that teachers should consider how they *sequence* questions depending on what purpose they want to accomplish. For example, they said that sequences that begin with a higher-level question and then move through lower-level follow-up questions may be appropriate for some purposes (such as asking students to suggest an application of an idea and then asking for details about how this application might work). In addition, they maintained that sequences of the opposite type—a series of lower-level questions followed by a higher-level question—would be appropriate for other purposes (such as calling students' attention to specific facts and then encouraging them to draw some conclusion from all the facts). Again, the main point here is that rather than asking questions in a random fashion, teachers should plan specific types of questions that are clearly sequenced and designed to accomplish clear objectives and lesson goals. I will return to the issue of how teachers can sequence questions later in this chapter.

My favorite taxonomy of teacher questions looks not only at their type but also at their function and divides questions into two main types: *echoic* and *epistemic* questions. *Echoic* questions seek repetition or confirmation of something while *epistemic* questions seek information of some sort (see Figure 5.1).

Figure 5.1   Teacher Question Types and Functions

1. *Echoic*	Comprehension checks	*All right? OK?*
	Clarification requests	*What do you mean?*
	Confirmation checks	*Did you mean . . .?*
2. *Epistemic*	Referential	*Why didn't you do your . . . ?*
	Display	*What's the opposite of up?*
	Expressive	*It is interesting, isn't it?*
	Rhetorical	*Why didn't you do that? Because you . . .*

SOURCE: Adapted from Ellis (1994).

We can compare the referential and display questions in this epistemic section with the open and closed type of questions that Barnes (1976) talked about. They are similar but not the same as display questions, which test the students' knowledge. Although display questions can be *closed* and referential questions *open,* the opposite is also possible for both. I like to use this taxonomy of the functions of teachers' questions for my own use when I am trying to discover the type of questions I ask in class.

THINKING ABOUT YOUR OWN CLASSROOM

Refer to the transcript you prepared of a lesson in answering the following questions:

- What percentage of total class time is devoted to your questioning?
- Based on the three different checklists of teacher questions presented in this chapter, which type of questions do you usually use in class—which type do you tend to favor?
- What is the function of the questions you ask in class?
- Do you plan the different types of questions you will ask before class? If not, why not?

WAYS OF DIRECTING QUESTIONS

The way teachers direct questions during their classes is also important. Teachers have several options available for direction when asking general questions in class:

- *Group.* One option is to ask the whole class a question and have students self-select when to answer. Students can vie for the teacher's attention by putting their hands up or by shouting out the answer. Although the latter is not recommended in many teacher education courses, it has its purposes—especially if some of the students are shy because then the pressure is off of them to answer in public. Can you think of other purposes for which you may want students to shout out the answer? Also, teachers can call on students who do not raise their hands to see why they think they cannot answer the question. It may be that they know the answer but do not want to answer in public.

- *Individual—named first.* Teachers have the option of calling a student's name first and then asking the question. This alerts the student that a question is coming his or her way: "Suzie, what do you think?" Brophy and Good (1991) suggested at least three situations in which it is better to call on a student before asking a question: (1) the teacher wants to draw an inattentive student back into the lesson, (2) the teacher wants to ask a follow-up question of a student who has just responded, or (3) the teacher is calling on a shy or anxious student who may be overly surprised if called on without warning.

- *Individual—named last.* Of course, if a teacher calls the student's name first, then he or she cannot be sure the student is following the lesson. Another strategy might be to ask the question first and then call a student's name. This way, teachers can monitor if a student has been following the lesson.

Generally, we all know that teachers should distribute questions widely rather than allow a few students to answer most of them because students learn more if they are actively involved in discussions than if they sit passively day after day without participating. In addition, questions normally should not be repeated because we may be teaching our students that they need not pay attention because teachers always repeat the question.

Characteristics of Good Teacher Questions

Although Brophy and Good (1991) suggested that a good teacher question really depends on context, we can say that a *good* question stimulates thought, has reason and focus, and can challenge while at the same time maintaining student engagement. Brophy and Good maintained that good questions are *clear, brief, natural, purposeful, sequenced,* and *thought provoking:*

- *Clear.* Clear questions describe the specific points to which students are to respond; vague questions leave too many different answers possible and can confuse the students. For example, if a teacher of English wants to call attention to the verb tense in a sentence on the board and asks, "What do you see here?" the students would not know exactly what was called for. It would be better to ask, "What tense is used in this clause?"

- *Brief.* Questions should be brief because the longer the question, the more difficult it is to understand. Students end up scratching their heads wondering what is required from them.

- *Natural.* Questions should be spoken in natural, simple language and should be adapted to the correct level of the class. Yes, teachers should challenge their students a bit by asking questions that make them apply what they know, but teachers should be careful not to frustrate their students by asking questions at a language level they do not understand.

- *Purposeful.* In order to ask purposeful questions that help achieve the lesson's objective, teachers must plan ahead and possibly write out these questions in advance to make sure they do not have to improvise too much during the lesson. Brophy and Good (1991) maintained that many improvised questions are irrelevant and confusing to the students.

- *Sequenced.* As teaching aids, questions must not only be planned in advance but also sequenced correctly in a lesson. Teachers use sequenced questions because they are looking for specific answers to each question and then integrating each answer with previously discussed material before moving on to the next question. For example, a teacher can say: "Now that we have identified the main properties of language, which do you think chimpanzees use to communicate to each other? Do they communicate in the same way as humans? Do they communicate in the same way as birds? Do birds communicate in the same way as humans?"

- *Thought provoking.* To say that good questions are thought provoking may seem obvious to most teachers, yet look at the number of factual questions we continue to ask in our classes that do not take much real thought to answer. Yes, factual questions are necessary to see if our students are processing the information correctly, but we must also include questions that make our students think for themselves.

One important point I should make about questioning is that the value of any question depends on how and why it is used by the teacher. For example, during whole class discussions, teachers must consider whether they really want students to share opinions or just to recite the answer. In order to structure and conduct discussions that call for student sharing of opinions, teachers must adopt a different role from the one they play in drill and recitation activities by assuming a less dominant and less judgmental role. This change of role may not be easy for some teachers who may fear that they are giving up control or will lose control of their classes. However there are some alternatives to questioning that teachers can use in order to sustain discussions, such as using declarative statements to directly introduce an idea for discussion (e.g., "Corn has increased in price."). Teachers can then continue with indirect questions about the same topic when responding to student answers, such as, "I wonder what makes you think that." Brophy and Good (1991) maintained that this type of an indirect question can reduce anxiety and may even stimulate further thinking. Of course, teachers who want to maintain a discussion format must also invite and relish student-generated questions, and if all else fails, teachers can just shut up and let the students take over the discussion.

CHARACTERISTICS OF UNPRODUCTIVE QUESTIONS

A "bad" or unproductive question is any question that causes students to offer unproductive responses. Brophy and Good (1991) and Groisser (1964) outlined four specific types of questions that teachers use that can be termed unproductive: *yes–no questions, tugging questions, guessing questions,* and *leading questions:*

- *Yes–no.* Of course, teachers can use yes–no questions as warm-ups for other questions, but some teachers use these excessively and students learn just to shout out one or the other answer because they have a 50% chance of being correct. Yes–no questions really encourage students to guess the answer. In addition, these types of questions do not tell the teacher if a student has any real understanding of a concept. They have their place but should be used only sparingly because of the guesswork factor involved.

- *Tugging.* Tugging questions, such as a teacher saying to a student to "Continue . . ." or "Well . . ." are statements that often follow an incomplete student response. The teacher usually wants to hear more from the student, but tugging questions do not help the student at all because many perceive that they are being pushed or nagged into providing the "right" answer. Brophy and Good (1991) suggested that if teachers want to stay with a student while he or she is attempting to answer, then it is better to provide some specific help with the answer, such as rephrasing or giving some clues. How many times did we hear from our own teachers when we were students questions such as "What else? Give me another reason." But we students did not know what else or have any more reasons! It is better for teachers to cue the students to a specific aspect of the information they are looking for.

- *Guessing.* Of course, the yes–no and tugging questions invite some guessing from our students, but teachers also ask obvious guessing questions that require students to guess because they do not have the facts, such as, "How far do you think it is from London to New York?" Although it is sometimes useful to ask guessing questions to stimulate a student's imagination, they should not be overused.

- *Leading.* Leading questions (such as "Don't you agree?") are not very useful because they invite the student to depend more on the teacher. Many students consider them meaningless because they are not being asked for their own opinions.

TEACHER WAIT-TIME

The final aspect of teacher questioning that I want to address in this chapter concerns what happens after the teacher asks the question and how long he or she waits for a student to answer. Good questioning behavior requires allowing students sufficient time to think about and to respond to questions. Rowe (1974) reported that the teachers she observed waited less than *one second* before calling on someone to respond. Furthermore, even after calling on a student, they waited only about *one second* for a response. Such teacher behavior does not make sense because teachers minimize the value of their questions by failing to give students time to think. Rowe followed up these observations by training teachers to extend their wait times from less than one second to three to five seconds. She discovered the following changes (as reported in Brophy & Good, 1991):

- Increase in the average length of student responses
- Increase in unsolicited but appropriate student responses
- Decrease in failures to respond
- Increase in speculative responses
- Increase in student-to-student comparisons of data
- Increase in statements that involved drawing inferences from evidence
- Increase in student-initiated questions

These results suggest that teachers may want to provide at least three seconds of thinking time after asking a question, as this seems to improve the chances of our students contributing to their own learning in our classes. If teachers continue to wait only one second, students become socialized into waiting *before* suggesting an answer because they know the teacher will provide the answer just to fill in the silence. One way I remind myself to wait at least three seconds is to pinch the skin on my hand.

THINKING ABOUT YOUR OWN CLASSROOM

- Listen to the recording of your teaching, and try to determine how long you wait for a student response after asking a question.
- How does your wait-time compare to the optimum wait-time described above? If you need to change yours, how do you plan to do that?

REFLECTING ON TEACHERS' QUESTIONS

Referring to the fundamental *IRE* pattern of classroom interaction, Cazden (1988) said that the initiation usually comes in the form of a question, and as such, teacher questions are one of the dominant forms of communication used in the classroom. Teachers use questions for most of their classroom communications as a means of checking that their students are following their lessons. Research has shown that many teachers may not be aware of the number or type of questions they ask in class or the function of those questions. In addition, many teachers may not be aware of the length of their wait-time after asking a question and the fact that a shorter wait-time leads to less student participation. Thus, it is important for teachers to be aware of the number of questions they ask, the type of questions they ask, the function of the questions they ask, and the amount of wait-time they practice after asking questions so that they can be as effective as possible in maintaining student interest and learning.

CHAPTER SIX

OK! Good!

Exploring Teacher Feedback

By providing feedback to students, teachers are expressing one of two things: the teachers like the response, or they do not like the response. In other words, feedback provides students with a measure of their current progress and tells them whether or not they need to improve in any way. Regardless of their age group, students are very savvy; they quickly learn how to read a teacher and the particular ways in which he or she provides feedback. For example, they can read the different meanings of *OK*. Students become used to a teacher's ways of providing feedback, such that when the teacher says, "Good," the students know whether the response was good or whether *good* was just a filler word. Of course, in the heat of the fast-paced classroom, it is difficult for teachers to monitor their use of this type of feedback because they are probably thinking about the next item they are about to teach. However, feedback of all kinds is a very important signpost for students because it tells them how they are doing. As teachers, we must ask ourselves, Does the type of feedback we provide reflect our beliefs and philosophy of learning and teaching? Unfortunately, many teachers remain unaware of the type and frequency of feedback they provide in their classes and the effect of this feedback on their students' progress and overall learning. This chapter explores different facets of teacher feedback and suggests strategies teachers can employ when providing feedback to and for their students.

PURPOSES OF TEACHER FEEDBACK

Teachers provide feedback to students with some different purposes in mind, such as providing *information* for both teachers and students, providing *advice* for students, providing students with *motivation,* and providing feedback that can lead to *student autonomy* (adapted from Lewis, 2002).

Information

Feedback is one way for teachers to tell their students what they are doing well and what they need to improve on. Feedback from students tells teachers how both individual students and the class as a whole are doing so that they can adjust their instruction accordingly. Thus, feedback provides an ongoing form of evaluation for both teachers (of their teaching) and students (of their progress), which is in addition to the information provided by the regular end-of-term grading system. This regular feedback can provide students with ongoing comparisons from week to week so that they can decide what they need to do to improve instead of waiting for their end-of-term grade.

Advice

Connected to the valuable information that feedback provides for both teachers and students is the follow-up of specifically advising students as to how they can improve their learning if it is deemed a problem. Teachers can follow up their feedback with suggestions for specific learning strategies that the students should incorporate into their learning; if possible, the teacher should model these strategies rather than just explain them (for a detailed example of this, please see Farrell, 2009). Lewis (2002) suggested that students keep learning journals in which they write to the teacher about the learning strategies they are using. The teacher then responds to the student, and the student in turn responds to the teacher's feedback and asks questions or requests any additional information.

Motivation

Depending on how it is presented, feedback can provide motivation for students by encouraging them to stretch their abilities to the fullest. However, feedback, as we all probably know from our own school days, can also be demotivating when it is presented in a demeaning manner in which the student is humiliated in some way. Feedback should encourage students of all abilities by providing specific pointers on how they can improve their learning. Teachers should give some indication or acknowledgment every time students respond to a question; otherwise, they will not bother to respond in the future. Lewis (2002) emphasized the importance of teachers providing feedback on what students are doing well, either individually or as a class. She provided the following examples of what a teacher can say after a class discussion:

- "Most of you knew how to take turns."
- "You introduced your ideas with phrases like 'That reminds me.'"
- "You linked your ideas to what other people had said."
- "It was good to hear people clarifying what others had said, using questions like 'Did you say . . . ?'"

Lewis (2002) also suggested that teachers make positive comments as feedback on how students are using learning strategies effectively, such as "I was pleased to see that you asked the other person to explain a difficult word."

Student Autonomy

If students are motivated to excel as a result of the feedback we provide, then they can become more autonomous learners. Surely this is one of our most important teaching objectives: that our students will no longer *need* our feedback because they have progressed to the point where they have become independent learners. Lewis (2002) compared this purpose of feedback with scaffolding: when a building is going up it needs scaffolding, but when it is finished, the scaffolding is taken away and the building can stand on its own. In the same way, we want our students to one day "stand on their own."

TEACHER FEEDBACK STRATEGIES

What happens when, after asking a question, teachers do not get the desired responses from their students? What strategies do they use when giving feedback? Research has indicated that teachers usually provide feedback to the student responses that follow most of the initiations that they make in class. Belleck, Kliebard, Hyman, and Smith (1966), for example, observed that when the teacher initiates and the students respond, 75% of the student responses are evaluated, and many of these evaluations are in the form of teacher repair where the teacher has to clear up some misunderstanding. Lewis (2002) asked, What do you do if a student provides the wrong answer? Do you ignore it (temporarily or permanently), correct the error of fact but not the form (or vice versa), prompt the speaker to find the error, ask someone else to find the error, correct and explain the error (each teacher will define errors according to his or her subject matter), or do something else entirely?

Generally speaking, when people provide any kind of feedback in communication they are giving the speaker the information that they are listening to what is being said, and it can be verbal (such as "OK" or "Really!") or nonverbal (such as a nodding of the head or a smile). This process of giving and receiving feedback is ongoing and can be positive (such as in the examples mentioned previously) or negative; when negative (such as a frown), the intent is to change the behavior or direction of the communication. Not many teachers realize that *OK* can have many different meanings, yet it is the most frequent comment teachers use after student responses in class (Fanselow, 1992). Fanselow (1992) provided the following examples of different feedback using *OK*. Try to come up with two different meanings of *OK* for each response and compare your answers with the answers below:

**1. Teacher to
student in
hall of school:**   Take off your hat!

Student in hall to teacher and peers: OK.

2. Teacher: How many elements are there in water?

Student: Two?

Teacher: OK.

   Possible Meanings:

1. First meaning: If you say so. Second meaning: Yes, sir.

2. First meaning: I heard you. Second meaning: I'm going to the
                  next student.

Did you come up with similar or different suggestions of possible meanings? If you came up with many different meanings, perhaps this is an indication of one of the reasons that *OK* is used so often by teachers—it can mean so many different things and the teacher is thinking on his or her feet. It is used so often, in fact, that it has little to do with indicating correctness. It may simply close a conversation, indicating we teachers are not sure what to say. For example, I think we can all use "OK. Very good" in a sarcastic manner—try it! The point here is that many teachers may not be aware of not only how they use *OK* in different ways, but how they provide feedback generally and how they sometimes confuse giving feedback with evaluating students. Civikly (1992), for instance, pointed out that whereas evaluation is judgmental and summative (occurs *after* an assignment), feedback is more descriptive and formative (occurs *during* an assignment).

THINKING ABOUT YOUR OWN CLASSROOM

Use the transcript of your own classroom communications to examine how you give feedback to your students:

- Did you notice any patterns in how you provide feedback?
- Do you use praise as feedback?
- If yes, how often do you use praise? Do you use praise too little or too often?
- What kind of praise do you use—do you say good or excellent or something else?
- Do you use *OK* as feedback, and how many different ways do you use it?
- How do you deal with sensitive students when giving feedback?

Teacher Elicitations

We can also look at teacher feedback in terms of elicitations. This method refers to the teacher's use of prompts (or questions) to draw out the desired response from the students. Elicitations can be divided into the following classifications (adapted from Tsui, 1992):

Elicit: Inform are questions that a teacher uses to invite students to supply a piece of information to obtain feedback. From the students' responses, the teacher can then find out whether the students know the answers he or she is looking for. The following example shows how a teacher can use *elicit: inform* to find out what the students know about vehicles and, specifically, trucks.

Elicit: Inform

1: Teacher: What do you know about cars? What about vehicles, does anyone know the meaning of the word *vehicle?*

2: Teacher: How about trucks? Who knows the meaning of the word *truck?*

Elicit: Confirm invites the addressee to confirm the speaker's assumption; in the classroom, many times teachers use this to obtain specific feedback that the students are indeed following the lesson. In the previous example, the teacher used these questions both to invite students to confirm his or her assumption that students had understood the meanings of *vehicle* and *truck* and to make sure they were ready to possibly use these in a sentence to show they knew the meaning. This is outlined in the example of *elicit: confirm* that follows.

Elicit: Confirm

1: Teacher: OK. So is everyone very clear on what a vehicle is and what a truck is? OK. Are you ready to make sentences with these words now?

Elicit: Agree invites the addressee to agree with the speaker's assumption. For *elicit: agree* questions, a teacher, for example, can use such questions to invite students to agree with his or her assumption that a specific proposal or suggestion is true. In the example that follows, the teacher (in two different turns, with Turn 2 more detailed than Turn 1) asks or invites her students to agree (or not) with the answers.

Elicit: Agree

1: Teacher: It's for transporting things, right?

2: Teacher: The truck brings things such as furniture. Right?

Elicit: Repeat invites the addressee to repeat (or clarify) what was previously said. The teacher asks students to repeat their previous utterances because either he or she has not heard their responses correctly or the students have said something important that he or she wants the rest of the class to listen to again. The example below outlines what happens when the teacher does not get a clear answer and provides feedback to invite students to repeat the response.

Elicit: Repeat

1: Teacher: What did you say just when . . . ?

[Students shout out something]

2: Teacher: OK! *[Facing the class.]* John, what did you say?

Feedback Language

The following framework of feedback strategies may be useful for teachers to consider implementing, especially when their feedback is in written form (adapted from Lewis, 2002):

- *Agree/disagree:* "I agree/disagree with the point you made about . . ."
- *Ask a question:* "Did you say . . . or . . ."
- *Express feelings:* "I am delighted to see that you . . ."
- *Generalize:* "Generally, your work is very good."
- *Provide examples:* "For example, your . . ."
- *Give reasons:* "I have marked your math in red because you need to . . ."
- *Provide comparisons:* "By the end of your speech you were really expressing yourself well."
- *Make an offer:* "Would you like to discuss your speech?"
- *Make a prediction:* "From this speech I can see that you will have no trouble with . . ."
- *State a plan:* "Next week we will . . ."
- *Make a suggestion:* "I would suggest that you . . ."

Of course, these strategies may seem obvious to many teachers, but it is useful for us to see them in writing so that we can use them as a checklist to reflect on how (and if) and how often we are using them.

THINKING ABOUT YOUR OWN CLASSROOM

Lewis (2002) provided the following results of a class observation on teacher feedback. In this class, the children were learning about sound-spelling relationships in English; the observer noted the following examples of feedback by the teacher to individual children (I only provide a few of these):

"Good."

"No."

"Say it again."

"I like the way people are putting their hands up. How many letters can you see?"

"How many sounds . . . ?"

"OK."

"All right. You sit on your bottom. Good."

"Short." [Repetition of one-word answer]

After the lesson, the observer summarized all the types of feedback and found that they seemed to fall into *five* categories:

1. Praise (Good, etc., or repetition of the child's answer)
2. Correction (No)
3. Requests for repetition (Say it again.)
4. Evaluation of behavior (that child's or someone else's)
5. Requests for further information (. . . and what sound does it make?)

Using the five categories as a checklist, look at the transcript of your lesson—specifically, look at each time you provided feedback to your students. See what percentage of each category you use and if you use any other categories.

REFLECTING ON TEACHER FEEDBACK

Teacher feedback is not as clear cut as it may seem because there are many different purposes for feedback and ways teachers can deliver it—and many different ways students are affected by such feedback. That said, the purpose of this chapter was to alert teachers to the many different meanings of teacher feedback and to provide teachers with different strategies they can consider when delivering feedback to students. As I suggested earlier, teachers need to become more aware of their own feedback strategies and their affect on student motivation and learning; the best way to accomplish this is by looking at classroom communication transcripts and specifically noting each time feedback is given. In this manner, teachers can then decide how they want to adjust their feedback strategies.

CHAPTER SEVEN

Two Heads Are Better Than One

Utilizing Learner Groupings

At many levels of my education, but especially in high school, I was not particularly pleased when the teacher broke us into pairs or groups. I thought it was a waste of time in certain instances, and I always relied on someone else in the group to come up with an answer for the teacher. That said, at the same time, I was always amazed that someone would come up with an answer and that the answer he or she came up with was really good. I am not sure, however, if the pair work or group work had had any real influence on that answer because the person who delivered it always embellished the "group" answer in some fascinating way. Some teachers (and probably students) may question the idea that *two heads are better than one* because some may think group work a waste of time. However, when people come together for a common purpose, and when they cooperate fully with each other, they can actually come up with some really good ideas—but this does not happen automatically, as will be pointed out in this chapter. When students are put into pairs or groups, they must interact and communicate more than is required when a teacher talks in front of the class. This can result in our students developing into more independent learners.

This chapter explores both the different types of communications and interactions generated by whole-class groupings, small groups, or pair work and how teachers can monitor such learner groupings so that they provide optimal opportunities for learning in their classrooms. Each of the learner-grouping arrangements requires different physical settings and especially different classroom seating arrangements (see Chapter 8 for a discussion of physical settings and their effects on classroom communication).

WHOLE-CLASS GROUPING

Whole-class grouping is probably the most common classroom learner arrangement—the students usually sit in rows, and the teacher is located at the front of the room. This type of learner grouping has both positive and negative effects on student learning. From a positive perspective, Richards and Lockhart (1994), among others, suggested that whole-class learning may actually be a more efficient way of instruction in situations where teachers have to deal with very large classes and have a limited time to teach a specific curriculum. They suggested that when the whole class is together, it can promote a sense of security among slower learners because they can rely on the faster learners to provide group answers until the slower learners catch up.

Whole-class grouping also has some negative effects on student learning. Harmer (1995) called whole-class grouping "lockstep" learning and explained: "All the students are 'locked into' the same rhythm and pace, the same activity . . . the traditional teaching situation, in other words, where a teacher-controlled session is taking place" (p. 243). In this arrangement, the teacher controls all of the communication and the class, regardless of how many students are in the room, is seen as only one group. In such an arrangement, students have few opportunities to interact with the teacher or with each other because of the amount of control the teacher asserts, not to mention that the seating arrangement (in rows) makes interaction unnatural. When teachers use a whole-class grouping arrangement, they are assuming (although I do not think most teachers are consciously aware of these assumptions) that *all* students proceed at the same learning pace. You are probably saying that of course we realize from our teaching experiences that we have students who can indeed follow the pace of our instruction, but we also have students who are slower and have different learning styles and use different learning strategies than the main group. And since we teachers teach the *whole* class, we always take these slower students into account. However, if we always use whole-class grouping for our instruction, we must also realize that our slower students may get left behind, not to mention that our faster students may become less interested in class because the teacher is probably teaching to the middle. All this may be lost and hidden to the teacher because he or she is probably monitoring the whole group and not individual student reactions.

TURN ALLOCATION IN WHOLE-CLASS GROUPING

When students enter school, they are exposed to classroom discourse patterns that may differ greatly from the normal conversational style used at home (as was pointed out in Chapter 2). Nevertheless, most teachers expect their students to be able to interact with the teacher and their peers, and in order to be viewed as competent learners, students must be able follow appropriate turn-allocation rules in the participation structure (Mehan, 1979).

In most whole-class, teacher-directed lessons, turn allocation occurs almost solely by the teacher selecting the next speaker through one of these processes:

1. *Individual nomination*—teacher calls on a specific student

2. *Group invitation to reply*—teacher calls on the whole class to reply

If these allocations break down in any way, the teacher may then choose to use one or more improvisational strategies to restore order in the turn-allocation process. These include (1) doing nothing, (2) getting through, (3) opening the floor, and (4) accepting the unexpected. However, these rules are not explicitly taught. Therefore, culturally and linguistically nonmainstream students may have special difficulty learning how to effectively participate in classroom communications.

In an interesting comparison of teacher-directed whole-group lessons in two third-grade classrooms with linguistically and culturally different students and teachers, Pamela McCollum (1989) looked at turn-allocation procedures and how they affected classroom participation structures. One class, in Chicago, Illinois, was composed of an English-speaking, mainstream American teacher and students; the other class, in Rio Piedras, Puerto Rico, had a Spanish-speaking teacher and students. These two classes had similar academic tasks, and McCollum suggested that classroom competency would be seen as students responding to the teacher's questions with correct academic information at the right time, following appropriate turn-allocation rules (i.e., students must speak within the *IRE* sequence). Her main reason for looking at these diverse groups of students in the two participation structures was to document difficulties nonmainstream students may have in learning to participate effectively in mainstream classrooms. I highlight the findings of this study because they have implications for all teachers in that the manner in which they set up turn-allocation procedures accounts for the different participation structures in their classes. Each teacher needs to know the cause and effect of these turn allocations. A summary of the different turn-allocation procedures in both the mainstream American classroom and the Puerto Rican classroom is shown in Figure 7.1.

Figure 7.1   Turn-Allocation Procedures in Two Different Classrooms

Mainstream American Classroom	Puerto Rican Classroom
• Organization of lesson closely followed traditional *IRE* sequence. • Teacher had strict control of student talk. • Talk focused on topic of lesson. • Teacher used individual nomination of students. • Teacher initiated interactions much more than the students did. • Teacher often ignored students' initiations.	• Organization of lesson closely followed variations in *IRE* sequence. • Teacher acted as a facilitator of classroom interaction. • Talk during lesson resembled everyday conversation. • Teacher used invitation to reply most frequently. • Ratio of student- versus teacher-initiated turns of talk was more equal. • Teacher frequently acknowledged students' initiations.

Mainstream American Classroom

The lesson in the mainstream American classroom in Chicago was typical of a traditional teacher-led lesson and followed the teacher-initiated *IRE* structure. The lesson was fast-paced, with the teacher maintaining strict control of student talk and keeping fully focused on the topic so as to fulfill her academic task. The teacher's frequent use of individual nomination of specific students enabled her to keep strict control over the pace and course of the lesson. The academic task structure was effectively and efficiently set up at the expense of social participation, as students' comments that were off-topic were often ignored. The social participation structure was a recitation-style classroom interaction whereby learning is unidirectional from teacher to the students and where teachers are seen as providers of information.

Puerto Rican Classroom

In complete contrast to the mainstream American classroom that followed a teacher-initiated *IRE* sequence, the Puerto Rican classroom was characterized by the teacher's responsiveness to student contributions. Learning was accomplished in a reciprocal fashion, with classroom communication more characteristic of a conversation between the teacher and the students. The teacher was open to student initiations and responded to each one. The ratio of teacher- and student-initiated turns of talk was relatively equal, with the "invitation to reply" procedure being used most frequently. All students were allowed to relate their personal experience to the text, and they had the freedom to interact with the teacher without strict turn-taking rules.

Implications for Teachers

The turn allocations in the two different classrooms may be summarized as follows:

Turn-Allocation Procedures *Chicago*	*Turn-Allocation Procedures* *Puerto Rico*

• *Individual nomination = 62%*
• *Invitation to reply = 24%*
• *Ignoring students'*
  initiations = 44%
	• *Individual nomination = 34%*
	• *Invitation to reply = 62%*
	• *Ignoring students'*
	  initiations = 8%

We can clearly see that each teacher had a different philosophy on how to conduct whole-group lessons and that the different types of student–teacher interaction were probably dependent on their beliefs about the roles of teachers and students regarding instruction and how learning is perceived to be best accomplished. In the Chicago classroom, which is probably representative of mainstream classrooms in the United States, the teacher mostly nominated specific students to reply during class, and the classroom communication structure was of a teacher-initiated, *IRE*, recitation style. We can probably say that the Puerto Rican classroom had a communication structure more similar to that of a *Talk Story* (Au & Jordan, 1981), which allows students to participate in instruction in culturally patterned ways that increase their participation in and comprehension of reading lessons. The use of more invitations to reply and less ignoring of students' initiations makes classroom communication seem more like everyday ways of speaking outside of school. As was already pointed out in Chapter 2, and as McCollum (1989) concluded, if the Puerto Rican students were to participate in a mainstream recitation-style classroom in the United States, their way of communicating might be deemed socially inappropriate and their behaviors erroneously diagnosed as indications of social (or even emotional) maladjustments because they are culturally and linguistically different from the mainstream.

What are the implications for us as teachers? We all need to realize that our expectations about the appropriate ways of speaking within our classrooms (i.e., the classroom participation structures) are not usually explicitly explained or taught to students on the first day of class; rather, many teachers assume that *all* their students know the rules of interaction in their classes. So there is an obvious and important need for teachers to *explicitly* outline their expectations and intentions with regard to the rules of turn taking in whole-class learner groupings. Connected to this is the need for teachers to allow for greater variability in academic task structures and social participation structures by providing culturally congruent instruction so as to maximize the competencies of nonmainstream learners. So rather than stifle our students' urges to contribute to the whole-class lesson, and rather than suppressing their thoughts by ignoring their initiations, maybe we should become more open to facilitating this type of communication structure in our whole-class grouping if we want to maximize the competencies of all our students. Of course, in order to know if we are stifling or suppressing our students in our classes, we need to first analyze the whole-class group and the teacher–student interactions to see what is actually occurring (as opposed to what we *think* may be occurring) using the data collection process described in Chapter 3. Then we can decide if we need to make any changes to our instructional and hence interactional teaching patterns.

THINKING ABOUT YOUR OWN CLASSROOM

- Under which classroom conditions do you favor whole-class grouping?
- Which turn-allocation procedures do you think best suit your classes and why?
- Based on the transcript of your own classroom communication, which pattern of turn allocation do you think your classes follow in whole-class grouping?
- Some educators maintain that in whole-class groupings, learning occurs through interaction and, as a result, the teacher should be a facilitator assisting the learners rather than directing them. Do you think the teacher should facilitate learning or direct/control learning? Explain the reasons for your answer.
- What is your opinion of the idea that students should have the freedom to interact with the teacher without strict turn-taking rules being enforced?

SMALL GROUPS/PAIR WORK

Implementation of small group or pair work in our classes, although it sounds good and we may think it easy to use, actually requires a paradigm shift for most teachers (Jacobs & Farrell, 2003). In order for teachers to implement small groups and pair work, they must be able to focus greater attention on the role of learners and be able to move from whole-class, teacher-centered instruction to learner-centered or learning-centered instruction. This also means that teachers must be able to focus greater attention on the learning *process* rather than on the final products that learners are supposed to produce (or move from product-oriented instruction to process-oriented instruction). Thus, if teachers want to use small group interaction in their classes, they must be ready to give up some of their power and control over their students in order for them to have a truly enriching learning experience. For this to happen, teachers must encourage *learner autonomy* and *collaborative learning* in their classrooms (Jacobs & Farrell, 2003).

Learner Autonomy

Learner autonomy involves "learners being aware of their own ways of learning, so as to utilize their strengths and work on their weaknesses" (Jacobs & Farrell, 2003, pp. 10–11). Group work and pair work provide opportunities for learner autonomy in that our students can learn how to access the quality of their own work within the pair or group; this lessens the threat of assessment being based solely on teacher evaluations. Thus, students working in pairs and groups can become self-dependent and self-motivated to learn because the teacher is no longer in total control and no longer solely responsible for student learning. We teachers are not entirely left out of the learning though and still maintain some responsibility for overall management of the learning environment. Even though learners are collaborating solely with their peers, and thus "move away from dependence on the teacher" (Jacobs & Farrell, 2003, p. 11), they do not completely dispense with the teacher as he or she needs to set the learner-autonomy process in motion in the first place. In addition, in order to enhance learning in pairs or groups, students need assistance from their peers that would not be available in whole-class activities, and this also calls for more collaboration with these same peers.

Collaborative Learning

Collaborative learning, also known as cooperative learning, consists of learners engaging in group activities that enhance student-student interaction. As Barnes (1976) reminded us, group work "only becomes possible when successful class discussions have reassured pupils that their contributions are valuable, both from the teacher's point of view and their own" (p. 130). For this to happen, the teacher must support the groups rather than abandon them with the hope that meaningful dialogue will just happen if you put the students together. One way a teacher can influence the groups is by teaching the students collaborative skills, such as disagreeing politely, asking for help, and giving examples and explanations (Jacobs & Farrell, 2003).

Many students may be unaccustomed to working with others on academic tasks. Thus, they may need to focus explicit attention on collaborative skills if they are to develop and deploy such skills. These skills are also vital language skills, skills that will serve students well in their future academic careers and in other aspects of their lives where they collaborate with others. (Jacobs & Farrell, 2003, p. 13)

Barnes (1976) pointed out that in order to set up small groups, teachers should consider the following:

- Begin with the students' feelings of competence.
- Establish a common ground so that students can reinterpret what the teacher says.
- Focus the students' attention on specific ideas.
- Pace the lesson not in terms of time, but in terms of type of language used (exploratory language).

MAKING GROUPS WORK

According to Barnes (1976), the success of a group depends on the level of interaction within that group. He suggested that this level of interaction depends on "the extent to which members of the group are genuinely working together, trying to communicate and understand" (p. 38). Such positive interdependence, according to Jacobs and Farrell (2003), helps students "feel support and belonging at the same time that they are motivated to try hard to assist the group in reaching its goals" (p. 12). Group discussions can end as quickly as they begin if the group takes a closed approach to accomplishing tasks, that is, if "the group finds nothing to encourage active engagement, nothing to provoke questions or surmises" (Barnes, 1976, p. 38). Teachers must therefore encourage group participants not to readily accept a persuasive member's words or make agreements just to satisfy that person's ego. This approach limits investigation and exploration of issues because probing questions that underlie an issue are not asked. Alternatively, Barnes (1976) suggested a more open approach to tasks within a group where students "ask probing questions, come to tentative decisions, and invite elaboration by others" (p. 67).

When learners are involved in group work, they need to develop strategies that build their higher-order thinking skills within the group, and this is sometimes also called critical and creative thinking skills (Jacobs & Farrell, 2003). I have found Bloom's Taxonomy of thinking skills very useful for guiding students when they want to apply and synthesize information in order to create something from that information (Bloom, 1956). This process can be represented as follows:

- *Analyze:* Break down information into parts by group discussion and make lists of the parts.
- *Synthesize:* Put together the ideas or parts into a new plan by group discussion.
- *Evaluate:* Evaluate the merit of the ideas or materials based on an agreed (by group) set of standards in the form of group discussion or debate.
- *Apply:* Put this plan into action by using the new accepted ideas or materials in new situations.

Thus, various thinking skills are called into play during group work as students attempt to explain concepts and procedures to their group members, as group members give each other feedback, and as they debate the proper course of action. Because of the absence of the teacher in group discussions, the students themselves must initiate, respond, and in certain cases evaluate or acknowledge responses and initiations made by other group participants. However, group work does not mean a complete absence of the teacher. In fact, the teacher remains central to the success of group work and project work (Johnson, 1995). The teacher can influence the success of the group by making sure that the task undertaken is appropriate and that the students all know what is expected from them during group work. The teacher may also want to monitor group discussions because these discussions may remain at the superficial level or may not be able to conclude successfully if they have no guidelines to follow for the discussions. Barnes (1976), however, warned against teacher intervention because he suggested that it may reduce the learning effect of the group work because the initiative is taken away from the group itself and the students may end up trying to do only what the teacher wants. "The very presence of the teacher alters the way in which pupils use language, so that they are more likely to be aiming at answers which gain approval than using language to reshape knowledge" (p.78). Therefore, in order for group learning to be effective, the teacher must control only two aspects of group work:

1. how learning goals are structured and

2. how conflicts within the group are resolved.

Johnson (1995) maintained that teachers structure the goal of learning in a group in one of three ways: cooperative, competitive, or individualist, with each one encouraging different patterns of group interaction and communication. For example, a cooperative group structure would promote positive collaboration among its members, whereas a competitive structure would foster a more cautious and defensive style of interaction and communication, and an individual type of group structure would encourage little, if any, student-to-student interaction and communication. Of course, there will inevitably be conflict within any group because individual members will not always agree about everything that is said or done. Looking at differences within a group in a positive way, Cazden (1988) said this conflict can challenge group members to rethink their initial ideas. She called this *Discourse as Catalyst* (p. 126). The teacher plays a large part in ensuring that this cognitive conflict within a group remains constructive rather than negative by making sure that the group members have learned strategies for solving their problems.

THINKING ABOUT YOUR OWN CLASSROOM

- Do you think small groups of three or pairs working together are better and why?
- Do you think small groups promote collaboration or disruption? Do they promote learner autonomy?
- If you have conducted group or pair work in your class, record communications in each type of group setting and transcribe it to determine what types of language are generated within the groups and pairs. Then compare interaction in both groups. This can be shared with the students too.
- Using the transcript, analyze what types of language are generated within the groups and pairs with and without teacher intervention.

REFLECTING ON LEARNER GROUPINGS

There is no one effective learner grouping that teachers can always use because decisions on whether to group learners as pairs, small groups, or as a whole class are usually best made according to the nature and purpose of the task at hand. Teachers should realize that they have different options available to them, rather than always following repetitive grouping and seating arrangements. Learner groupings influence peer relations and learner autonomy as well as student achievement. Teachers should examine their classroom transcript to reflect on the different communication patterns that exist in the different learner groupings they set up so that they can provide maximum learning experiences for their students.

CHAPTER EIGHT

I See What You're Saying

*Recognizing Nonverbal
Communication in the Classroom*

So far, we have only focused on spoken communications in the classroom and how teachers can reflect on and assess these communications to see if they are providing or blocking opportunities for student learning. Of course, there is another type of communication that occurs in all classrooms—nonverbal communication—and it is also a very important aspect of *talking, listening,* and *teaching.* However, both teachers and students are not always consciously aware of the power of their nonverbal communications in their classes. For example, when a teacher says to a student, "I see what you are saying," he or she may not realize it but that is exactly what is going on in terms of interpreting what the message really means. This is because the teacher is looking at the student's cues that are provided by nonverbal behaviors such as facial expressions, eye contact (or lack of eye contact), gesture, posture, and other body movements. Indeed, a noted researcher on nonverbal communication even suggested that "no more than 30 to 35% of the social meaning of a conversation or an interaction is carried by words" (Birdwhistle, 1970, p. 158).

As Stevick (1982) put it, "If verbal communication is the pen which spells out details, nonverbal communication provides the surface on which the words are written and against which they must be interpreted" (p. 163). In this chapter, attention is restricted to nonverbal behavior that has specific functions of communication. It is important for teachers to be able to control their own nonverbal communication and to be able to read their students' nonverbal signals in the classroom. This chapter outlines what nonverbal communication is and how teachers can learn to recognize it, control it, and use it to complement verbal communications so that they can provide an optimum learning environment for their students. The best way for teachers to monitor their nonverbal classroom behavior is to videorecord their classes, watch the recording, and note when, how, and why they use nonverbal behaviors and ask themselves if these behaviors are useful or not in maintaining an effective classroom learning environment.

FUNCTIONS OF NONVERBAL COMMUNICATION

Nonverbal communication has functions that include self-presentation, emotional and attitudinal expression, information processing, and interaction management. Civikly (1992) maintained that how others perceive us is directly related to how we present ourselves to them— especially in the nonverbal messages we emit, such as our physical appearance and how we use posture, gestures, and facial expressions when we communicate. From all our self-presentation in these ways, we will be deemed competent and trustworthy (or not!). In addition, and as already mentioned, we use more than words to express our attitudes and emotions, and these are evident in nonverbal communications such as tone of voice, facial expressions, eye gaze, and our use of gestures. Our making and responding to messages concerns our ability to process information, and we use many different nonverbal behaviors to facilitate both the sending and receiving of messages. When sending messages, for example, we may pause, change the volume, and use rhythm and different gestures to convey the importance of certain aspects of our message. Also, we respond to messages with certain facial expressions and gestures that tell the messenger what we think of the message. Of course, nonverbal communication also has a practical purpose in managing conversational turn taking and turn yielding.

That said, we must not forget that nonverbal communication does not occur in a vacuum but, rather, usually occurs alongside verbal messages. When nonverbal behaviors occur with verbal behaviors, the nonverbal behavior may reinforce or even contradict the verbal message. It is more common that the nonverbal behavior reinforces a verbal message. However, when the nonverbal behavior contradicts a verbal message, the recipient tends to see sarcasm in the message—especially if the communication is over- or understated. We must be cautious when interpreting the meaning of nonverbal behaviors because they may have multiple meanings (as do many of the words we use) depending on where they are used (context), how they are used, and who uses them. For the latter, a detailed knowledge of the person may be required before we can conclude the meaning of the nonverbal behaviors he or she may use.

Types of Nonverbal Communication

Nonverbal communication, as it is discussed in this chapter, focuses mainly on kinesics and proxemics. *Kinesics* deals with behaviors such as facial expressions, eye contact and eye expression, body movement, gesture and posture, and body shape and touch, while *proxemics* deals with personal space, seating arrangements, and the general environment. Other categories of nonverbal communication that are important, but that space issues preclude me from discussing in this chapter, include paralinguistic communication that deals with voice issues (pitch, tone, rhythm). However, I think that teachers may be able to read their students' voice characteristics and that students know when a teacher's tone and voice-rate change and the different associated meanings.

Kinesics

Let us look first at kinesics. Knapp and Hall (1992) suggested that kinesics consists of gestures, posture, touching behaviors, facial expressions, and eye behaviors. Some researchers suggest that humans have universal features of expression, at least when we are born (Ekman, 1982), while others suggest that our expressions are not based on evolution but socialization (Birdwhistle, 1970). This nature (we are born with these traits) versus nurture (we learn these traits after birth) difference is also present in the discussion on how humans learn to talk, so I will not get into it in any great detail in this chapter other than to say, as Pennycook (1985) suggested, "The safest position to take in this argument seems to be that certain types of expressive behavior, such as perspiring or pupil dilation, depend on the autonomic system and are presumably innate, but for most other forms of nonverbal communication, the expressive meaning differs across cultures" (p. 262). This chapter takes the position that there is probably a mixture of nature and nurture when it comes to nonverbal behaviors such as gestures and facial expressions.

Gestures

Birdwhistle (1970) maintained that the gestures that people in the United States use are composed of 57 different facial movements (or *kinemes*), 4 degrees of eyelid closure, and 3 different head nods, not to mention the many different movements and postures of the head, neck, trunk, shoulders, arms, wrists, hands and fingers, hips, legs and ankles, and the way we walk.

A child's use of gestures develops with age, and Neil (1991) distinguished between *iconic* gestures, which represent something in the physical world, and *metaphoric* gestures, which represent abstract ideas and seem to appear later than iconic gestures, at age 9. In young children, iconic gestures merge into mime. McNeill (1992) said that a preschool child describing a movement will usually turn his or her whole body around while describing it, as if following the moving object with his or her eyes, but an adult describing the same movement will usually only make a hand gesture, which he or she will not follow visually. So young children's use of gestures is centered on the self (like their speech), while adults are usually more detached when it comes to gestures. McNeill (1992) also described the ability of adults to return to a gesture after an aside.

In addition, we should also remember that gestures differ cross-culturally—especially when one thinks of greetings in different countries, and handshakes in particular. Pennycook (1985) reported on a study, for example, that identified seven different handshakes in East Africa that varied according to respect, age, and friendliness. Now compare this study of handshaking with what we can see on the streets in North America and how different ethnic groups have different ways of greeting each other and different accompanying handshakes.

Facial Expressions

If we take the same stance on the origin of facial expressions as we did with gestures, then we can say that facial expressions move from an initial biologically influenced mechanism (nature) to one which is influenced by socialization and individual learning and experience (nurture). Neil (1991) suggested that between the ages of 5 and 9, a child's ability to copy facial expressions improves quickly and that by the time they get to high school, most students can consciously control facial expressions in a manner that can make them unrelated to true feelings. An interesting example of the nature and nurture development of facial expressions is how a child in western culture develops his or her use of dominance signals (Neil, 1991). If we look at young children, we can see two signals used in interpersonal disputes: dominance ("plus face"—chin up and gaze at the opponent—and "looking down one's nose"), and subordination ("minus face"—chin down). Neil (1991) maintained that with age, *dominant* children come to use the chin in nonsocial situations, for example, when trying to tackle some difficult piece of equipment, and they show this by giving off a look of competence even before anything has taken place. In contrast, less dominant children (Neil calls these "unpopular children," but I would not go this far) give off signals of a different kind that indicate that they are not competent, again even before they start the interaction. This information is very important because children and teachers assess newcomers (both student and teacher newcomers) in the very first interactions and develop views of competence based on these first interactions that may not be fully appropriate but may leave a lasting impression. Thus, we humans do not seem to have much control over our nonverbal behaviors (though we do seem to have more control over our verbal behaviors), and as Pennycook (1985) pointed out, this "nonverbal leakage may often reveal what words do not" (p. 264).

THINKING ABOUT YOUR OWN CLASSROOM

- If you have videorecorded yourself teaching, review the recording and notice what kinds of gestures you use. What kinds of facial expressions do you use?
- Have you ever asked your students to mimic your use of gestures, and if yes, what did this reveal to you about your use of gestures?
- Have you ever asked your students to mimic your facial expressions, and if yes, what did this reveal to you about your use of facial expressions?

Proxemics

Proxemics is the study of space arrangements, space judgments, and interaction, and Hall (1966) named four different types of distance involved in interactions: intimate, personal, social, and public. Hall reminded us again that these differ greatly across cultures, with "high-contact" cultures (e.g., Arab, Hispanic) differing greatly from "low-contact" cultures (e.g., North American, Japanese). Proxemics looks, then, at room layout and general use of space and at peoples' attitudes toward space in public places—and especially at different cultures' interpretations of crowding and its affect on social behavior. For example, Americans' concept of proximity to others in public is much different from that of attitudes towards touching and proximity in Japan. In Japan's crowded streets, where touching in unavoidable, no apology is required; however, when touch occurs in public with a stranger in North America, an apology is required, though touch with friends is acceptable. Another interesting example is that touch between same-sex people is more acceptable in some cultures (e.g., Korean, Japanese, Puerto Rican) but less acceptable in others (e.g., North American); however, touch between opposite sexes in public is not common in these same cultures (except in appropriate ways, such as young couples in love!). This has implications for the classroom.

Hall (1966) also distinguished between sociopetal and sociofugal arrangements of space, with sociopetal arrangements being more conducive to communication between people and sociofugal arrangements emphasizing solitariness. Pennycook (1985) suggested that seating arrangements in cafes would be of the sociopetal type, while seating arrangements in waiting rooms at the doctor's office would be in a sociofugal arrangement. Space arrangements play an important role in the classroom. This is especially true when teachers are trying to arrange classroom space to encourage an optimal learning environment for their students.

As we saw in Chapter 7, teachers can group students for effective instruction in many different ways that include whole-group instruction (the entire class grouped together), small-group instruction (subgroups made up according to ability, interest, etc.), and individualized instruction (students work alone). Each grouping requires different physical settings (and especially different classroom seating arrangements). In an early study of teaching, Adams and Biddle (1970) discovered that many teachers (and most students) are unaware of the impact of the physical setting of the classroom on student-participation rates. They discovered that teachers who are more student-centered tend to design informal seating patterns that include circular or horseshoe (U-shaped) arrangements. On the other hand, they discovered that teachers who are more subject-centered tend to have a more traditional formal seating pattern that consists of students sitting in rows directly facing the teacher.

Closely connected to the arrangement of classroom space is the teacher's own use of space in the classroom and its influence on classroom participation. Powell and Caseau (2004) suggested that in the traditional classroom there is a zone of classroom participation where most interaction takes place, and this is from the middle in the front and down the middle rows, so that "students sitting on the sides and in the back do not receive as much attention and do not engage in as much interaction" (p. 11). Duncan and Biddle (1974) discovered that students who sit in the center of the room seem to be the most active participants (called "responders" in their study) and that verbal interaction was concentrated in this area of the classroom with the teacher in front of the room. Duncan and Biddle called this space the teacher's "action zone," and it is defined as the classroom space where specific students get the full focus of a teacher's attention through such nonverbal behaviors as eye contact and gaze and verbal behaviors such as questioning and nomination (Richards & Lockhart, 1994). Richards and Lockhart (1994) maintained that how narrow or wide a given teacher's action zone is may depend on the physical layout of the classroom—how the desks are placed (rows, semicircular, etc.). The teacher's action zone may also depend on how mobile a teacher is and also individual teacher preferences (personal action zone) and predispositions to look at one side of the class more than the other, or to call on one gender, ethnic group, or skilled learner over another. The main point of looking at proxemics in the classroom is to see if a teacher's action zone appears to favor or put at a disadvantage particular learners in any way and to gauge if the learners in the class appear to be happy or not with the extent to which they fall within or outside of the teacher's action zone. We must also remember that there is no single seating arrangement that is ideal for all classes.

THINKING ABOUT YOUR OWN CLASSROOM

- What is your classroom space philosophy?
- Draw the layout of your current classroom. Did you influence this layout?
- Now draw a design for your ideal classroom.

  - What are the main differences between your present classroom and your ideal classroom?
  - What changes can you make to your present classroom to improve the design?
  - Review a videotape of yourself teaching to determine your personal teaching action zone.
  - Do you tend to look to one side (right/left) more than to the other?
  - Do you tend to nominate learners of one gender more than those of the other?
  - Do you tend to nominate learners of one ethnic background more than those of another?
  - Do you tend to nominate only learners whose names you remember?
  - Do you tend to nominate mainly students at the front or the brightest students?

TEACHERS' USE OF NONVERBAL BEHAVIORS IN THE CLASSROOM

Classrooms differ from other social settings in that they are supposed to be about learning: teachers teach and students learn. However, students exert a strong influence over classroom processes (Neil, 1991). People who have spent any amount of time in a staffroom will tell you that when teachers come in after a class, they can be joyful or downtrodden because of the way they have perceived that class. Some typical teacher comments that can be heard include: "Oh, my students looked so happy with class today," or "My students looked so out of it today," or "When I ask a question, I can always tell when they don't know the answer because they either look out the window or stare down at their notes." These three comments show that teachers are using their students' body communications as an indicator that they are thinking in one direction or another. Of course, our students also have typical comments of their own regarding how the teacher looks: "She never smiles when I talk, but when Susan talks she always smiles" or "Even though he said it was OK, he did not seem to mean it."

Unfortunately, teachers do not readily reflect on their nonverbal behaviors, but these nonverbal behaviors may be very meaningful to their students (Civikly, 1992). That teachers have a tendency not to consider their nonverbal behaviors is not too difficult to understand. The classroom is a complex environment where the teacher has to deal with 20 to 30 students at the same time, and the pace moves so fast that many teachers feel overwhelmed with all they have to attend to. Thus, some may wonder why they should waste precious time reflecting on their nonverbal behaviors. I say this is definitely not a waste of time because when teachers have knowledge of and gain control over nonverbal communications and behaviors, it can help them teach better because they can learn to use communication modes besides just speaking. At the same time, they can become more aware of their students' nonverbal behaviors by learning to read their facial expressions, eye contact, vocal messages, body movements and gestures, personal space, touch, and physical appearances.

In comparison to verbal behaviors, most nonverbal behaviors occur at a lower level of conscious awareness, and people are usually surprised to learn how they come across to others. Neil (1991) pointed out that various studies have shown the value of a teacher's knowledge of nonverbal signals because elementary school teachers spent 78% of their time interacting verbally, while students spent 84% of their time not interacting at all, and this is similar for nonverbal behaviors in the classroom. For example, teachers usually teach (talk) to the whole class, especially when attempting to communicate complex ideas. However, that same teacher really does not have the time to verbally check that each student has understood what was explained, and constant interruptions are more than likely to disrupt the flow. Since the students are used to the conventions of whole-class teaching, they will not interrupt even when they do not understand something. If this is the case, then the teacher must rely heavily on assessing whether students understand from their facial expressions. However, assessing students' responses from their facial expressions may be problematic. For example, if a student yawns in class, does this mean the student is bored, or tired, or something completely different? In fact, Neil (1991) maintained that young students may not be able to communicate nonverbally as adults do or in a manner that is clearly understood by teachers.

Neil (1991) found that teachers use various nonverbal signals to communicate with and control their classes. Teachers might like to consider the following nonverbal behaviors when trying to restore classroom control:

- Use extended eye contact
- Shake head to indicate "no"
- Use facial expressions of disapproval
- Make a vocalization such as clearing the throat or a "shhh"
- Use gestures to put off the behavior
- Move closer to the site of the disruption
- Make use of approval facial expression when order is restored

---

THINKING ABOUT YOUR OWN CLASSROOM

- What is your opinion of the list of nonverbal behaviors that a teacher can use to restore control? Can you add more?
- Based on a review of a videotape of yourself teaching, what nonverbal behaviors do you use when trying to control your class? To control a sudden disruption? To show approval once order is restored?

REFLECTING ON NONVERBAL COMMUNICATION

The power of nonverbal communication is best captured by what Abercrombie (1968) mentioned some time ago, that although we speak with our vocal organs, "we converse with our whole body" (p. 55). Nonverbal communication is important in the classroom because both teacher and students may believe the nonverbal rather than the spoken message and because some messages can be conveyed implicitly by nonverbal means and would be unacceptable if they were sent through more explicit channels. In some cases, nonverbal signals may be the only ones available, for example, if a child is working at the other side of the room, or the teacher is working with a group and cannot talk to individuals. Nonverbal communication can become a real issue when we introduce cultural differences because students from different cultural backgrounds may have different interpretations for nonverbal communication. Thus, it is important for teachers and students to be aware that we communicate in many more ways than just by using words.

CHAPTER NINE

Professional Development

Reflecting on Classroom Communication and Interaction

Throughout this book, classroom communication is discussed and analyzed not only in terms of what actually occurs in the classroom (the language that is produced) but also in terms of what the teachers and students bring (beliefs, prior knowledge and experiences, and their cultural backgrounds) to this communication because both influence and shape the classroom language and interaction that ensues. That said, the main responsibility for shaping the type of classroom communication that occurs in each lesson lies firmly with the teacher because of his or her status and authority in this role. Thus, when we consider that teachers have already spent well over 14,000 hours sitting in these classrooms as students, plus the endless number of hours they continue to spend in the classroom as teachers, we can see that they have a vested interest in understanding what shapes communication in the classroom. Indeed, it is also important for administrators and even parents to fully understand the impact of classroom communication on learning because as Christie (2002) suggested, since "schools play such a powerful role in the contemporary world in apprenticing the young, their methods and procedures in achieving their particular kinds of symbolic control deserve our closest scrutiny" (p. 162). So as a teacher, your particular classroom and the accompanying classroom communication deserves your closest scrutiny so that you can make informed decisions about your teaching. As Briscoe, Arriaza, and Henze (2009) maintained, language used in classrooms can perpetuate inequities, and sometimes teachers can experience a phenomenon they called "catching [one]self." That is, the "words would fly out of the [teachers] mouths out of habit before they realized that those words did not match the beliefs they held" (p. 36).

Thus, teachers need to become more aware of how communication functions in their classrooms and the possibility that not *all* of our students know how to participate in this communication so that they can engage in optimum learning. Unfortunately, not many teachers are consciously aware of the communication and interaction patterns that currently exist in their classrooms and the effects of these patterns on student achievement. Are these patterns actually providing opportunities for students to learn? Or are they in fact blocking opportunities for students to learn? It is important for teachers to explore and study classroom communication because in doing so, teachers can see how patterns of communication have been established in their classes, the effect of these patterns on student participation, and how this participation shapes the way teachers use (or misuse) language for classroom learning.

REFLECTIVE PRACTICE AS PROFESSIONAL DEVELOPMENT

Reflective practice is seen as an approach to teacher professional development that is based on the belief that experienced teachers can improve their understanding of their own teaching by consciously and systematically reflecting on their teaching experiences (Farrell, 2007). The key to reflecting on classroom communication patterns in the manner they have been addressed in this book is that the teacher must gather concrete data about classroom communications to make informed decisions about their teaching. The most important type of concrete data a teacher should get is in the form of classroom transcripts, as suggested in Chapter 3. The teacher collects this type of data by placing an audio recorder or video recorder in his or her classroom. Once the data have been collected, the teacher then needs to transcribe the part of the recording that relates to the focus of the investigation. For example, teachers can transcribe only parts of their lesson, such as the opening or the closing, each time they give instructions, each time they ask a question, or whatever part of the lesson they are interested in. After this transcribing, the teacher can analyze and interpret the transcript as outlined in Chapter 3. After making interpretations about the communications that exist in their classes, teachers can decide if these are the types of communications and interactions that facilitate learning.

The purpose of this book is to provide a framework for novice and experienced teachers that may be useful when reflecting on and managing classroom communication and interaction in today's complex classrooms. This framework is based on the premise that both teachers and students bring prior experiences and beliefs to the classroom and that by a process of reflecting on these classroom communications teachers can become more aware of how the verbal messages, and the symbols we use to communicate, play a dramatic role in the classroom (Powell & Caseau, 2004). In the following sections, I discuss the interconnected ways teachers can engage in professional development through reflective practice.

Engage in Group Discussions

One way to begin the reflection process is to get a group of interested teachers to come together to talk about their teaching—especially the communication patterns they see existing in their classes. All the group members have to be equally responsible for keeping the group on track, so the group should negotiate when, where, and how often they want to meet. They should also negotiate an agenda for each meeting and distribute responsibilities evenly between the members.

Engage In Classroom Observations and Discussions

The group of teachers can decide to engage in classroom observations along with audio- or videorecording their classes so that they can see and hear the exact interactions and communications that take place in specific classes and gauge their effect on learning. Observation can be carried out alone, as in self-observation, pairs (as in critical friendships) can observe each other's classes, or the group can try to observe each member's classes in turn. That said, I suggest that classroom observations should start with the teachers looking at their own classroom communication patterns and interactions. For example, participants can tape their own classes and transcribe the parts of the tape that they are interested in investigating (as outlined in Chapter 3). In this way, the teachers can develop more confidence in describing their own teaching to others (especially to parents and administrators) because they have specific evidence in the form of recordings and transcripts, and they can also bring these to their group discussions with other teachers.

Engage in Journal Writing

Journal writing can also be carried out alone in the form of a diary, in pairs writing to and for each other, or in the group writing to and for each other. I suggest that teaching journals provide teachers with a written record (evidence) of various aspects of their practice, such as classroom events and interaction, and allow teachers to step back for a moment to reflect on these issues (Farrell, 2007). When teachers write regularly in a teaching journal, they can accumulate information that on later review, interpretation, and reflection can assist them in gaining a deeper understanding of the types of communication and interaction that occur in their classes. These journals can then be shared with the members of the teacher group, and the other members can comment orally or in writing. In addition, the group may want to collaborate to write a group journal with all members taking turns adding excerpts about classroom communication and interaction. This type of collaboration may raise more questions about important issues concerning aspects of communication and interaction that may not normally occur if writing a journal alone. For example, the following is an example of a summary of a teaching journal that outlines the sequence of classroom events (Farrell, 2007):

- Started class as usual
- Went over homework
- Noticed that most students did not do the homework
- Was annoyed and frustrated

The journal then goes on to explain each event in detail. If this class had been recorded, then the teacher and the group could have examined specific examples of the language used in the class (by both the teacher and the students) to see if there were any interesting patterns of communication. For example, the teacher and the group could transcribe the part of the communication that showed when the teacher noticed that most students did not do their homework and also map the interaction to see if he or she or the group could discover any underlying causes that might trigger insights about the class.

Of course, there are many ways teachers can engage in professional development other than the three outlined above, but I have found that these three can be the most productive.

THINKING ABOUT YOUR OWN CLASSROOM

The following reflections can be carried out alone, in pairs, or with your teacher group. In addition, you can write your answers in your teaching journal for yourself and to share with your peers or group. I have divided the questions into sections that may be useful for you because it may be a bit overwhelming to try to reflect on these questions all at once:

Teacher and Student Expectations

- What do/can/should you, as a teacher, expect of your students in terms of classroom communications (e.g., asking questions, answering questions, speaking in whole-class groups, in small groups, following instructions)?
- What do/can/should you, as a teacher, expect of yourself when giving instructions, asking questions, answering questions, setting up groups, engaging in nonverbal communication, giving feedback, giving praise, and so on?
- What do you think a student can/should expect from a teacher when dealing with classroom communication and interactions?
- What do you think a student can/should expect of himself/ herself when considering various aspects of their classroom communications and interactions?
- Briscoe, Arriaza, and Henze (2009) maintained that in a school environment, we have "words not only for the things that are important in that environment—such as desks, whiteboards, and computers—but also for classifications of people such as

students, teachers, administrators" (p. 19). What words do you and your students use for different classifications in your classroom and school, and are all these words appropriate?

Classroom Communication and Interaction Patterns

- How is communication and interaction set up in your class?
- Does the communication in your classroom follow the unmarked *IRE* structure or are there any variations in your lessons? Can you notice any other patterns in your classroom communications?
- Who has decided the patterns of communication and interaction in your classes?
- What are the effects of these patterns of communication and interaction on student participation?
- How do these patterns change in your classes (or do they change)?
- How do the students learn these?
- Do your classroom teaching behaviors match your stated intentions and beliefs about classroom communication and interaction?
- Language becomes transformative when it offers alternatives to the status quo and incorporates them into ways of thinking and discourse, thereby carving out new or different categories, relationships, and ways of representing the world, and opening up the possibility of transformative practices (Briscoe, Arriaza, & Henze, 2009). Do you think that the language used in your classroom can be described as being transformative? If so, can you give some examples of this type of language?

Teacher Questions and Feedback

- For what amount of class time is your communication in the form of questions?
- How many questions do you ask?
- What kind of questions do you ask?
- Which questioning strategies do you regularly find yourself following?
- How long is your wait-time after asking a question?
- What kind of feedback do you give?
- How do you evaluate your students?

Culture

- Do you notice any of your students who may be interacting using high-context messages (where much of the meaning is implied)?
- If yes, transcribe exactly what the communication is from these students.
- Can you explain the cultural backgrounds of all your students?
- How similar or different are their cultural backgrounds, and how do these similarities or differences effect classroom communication and interaction in your classes?

Classroom Nonverbal Communication

As discussed in Chapter 8, nonverbal communication in the classroom can be classified under the following headings: (1) environmental factors, (2) physical appearance, (3) proxemics, (4) kinesics, and (5) paralanguage. If you have audio- and videotaped your class, try to examine each aspect of nonverbal communication that occurs in your class. Here are a few questions to consider:

- What is the physical setting of your classroom and how does this affect interaction and communication?
- What is the zone of participation in your classes?
- What do you notice about teacher and student posture, gestures, facial expressions, eye behavior, and touching in the class?
- What do you notice about paralanguage or the nonlinguistic features of speech, such as volume, tempo, pitch, intensity, and accent?
- Do you notice any students who may be suffering from communication apprehension?

REFLECTING ON CLASSROOM COMMUNICATION AND INTERACTION

Communication plays a central part in today's complex classrooms, and as such, it is in a teacher's best interest to be able to recognize the communication patterns and interactions that occur in his or her classroom. As Powell and Caseau (2004) stated, classroom communication processes play a "significant role in the way instructional processes are managed" (p. 8). As such, a teacher needs to be able to recognize the social and interactional norms of his or her class in terms of who talks when and to whom and if his or her students come from backgrounds that may differ from such norms. It may in fact be difficult to give an exact definition of classroom communicative competence that is acceptable in all classrooms because it depends on the beliefs and practices of the teacher, the students, the classroom events, and the context of the schooling. Nevertheless, all meaningful instruction must account for the sociocultural and linguistic backgrounds of all our students. In this book, I have outlined a brief glimpse of the nature of classroom communication and why it is important for teachers to reflect on it. Knowledge about these patterns may help you make more informed decisions about your teaching so that all your students may experience a truly effective learning environment. Thank you for teaching, and thank you for reading this book.

References

Abercrombie, D. (1968). Paralanguage. *British Journal of Disorders of Communication, 3*, 55–59.

Adams, R. S., & Biddle, B. J. (1970). *Realities of teaching: Explorations with video tape*. New York: Holt, Rinehart, and Winston.

Allwright, D., & Bailey, K. M. (1991). *Focus on the language classroom: An introduction to classroom research for language teachers*. Cambridge: Cambridge University Press.

Au, K. (1980). Participation structures in a reading lesson with Hawaiian children: Analysis of a culturally appropriate instructional event. *Anthropology and Education Quarterly, 11*, 91–115.

Au, K. H.-P., & Jordan, C. (1981). Teaching reading to Hawaiian children: Finding a culturally appropriate solution. In H. T. Trueba, G. P. Guthrie, & K. H.-P. Au (Eds.), *Culture and the bilingual classroom: Studies in classroom ethnography* (pp. 139–152). Rowley, MA: Newbury House.

Barnes, D. (1976). *From communication to curriculum*. Middlesex, UK: Penguin.

Belleck, A., Kliebard, H., Hyman, R., & Smith, F. (1966). *The language of the classroom*. New York: Teachers College Press.

Biggs, A. P., & Edwards, V. (1991). "I treat them all the same": Teacher–pupil talk in multiethnic classrooms, *Language and Education, 3*, 161–176.

Birdwhistle, R. (1970). *Kinesics in context*. Philadelphia: University of Pennsylvania Press.

Bloom, B. S. (Ed.). (1956). *Taxonomy of educational objectives: Classification of educational goals. Handbook 1. cognitive domain*. New York: David McKay.

Briscoe, F., Arriaza, G., & Henze, R. C. (2009). *The power of talk: How words change our lives*. Thousand Oaks, CA: Corwin.

Brophy, J. E., & Good, T. L. (1991). *Looking in classrooms* (5th ed.). New York: HarperCollins.

Cazden, C. (1988). *Classroom discourse: The language of teaching and learning*. Portsmouth, NH: Heineman.

Christie, F. (2002). *Classroom discourse analysis: A functional perspective*. London: Continuum.

Civikly, J. M. (1992). *Classroom communication: Principles and practice*. Dubuque, IA: W. C. Brown.

Duff, P. A. (2002). The discursive co-construction of knowledge, identity and difference: An ethnography of communication in the high school mainstream. *Applied Linguistics, 23*(3), 289–322.

Duncan, M. J., & Biddle, B. J. (1974). *The study of teaching*. New York: Holt, Rinehart and Winston.

Edwards, D., & Mercer, N. (1989). Reconstructing context: The conventionalization of classroom knowledge. *Discourse Processes, 12*, 91–104.

Ekman, P. (1982). *Emotion in the human face*. New York: Cambridge University Press.

Ellis, R. (1994). Second language acquisition research and teacher development: The case of teachers' questions. In D. Li, D. Mahony, & J. Richards (Eds.), *Exploring second language teacher development* (pp. 175–194). Hong Kong: City University.

Erikson, F. (1982). Classroom discourse as improvisation. In L. C. Wilkinson (Ed.), *Communicating in the classroom* (pp. 153–181). New York: Academic Press.

Fanselow, J. (1987). *Breaking rules*. New York: Longman.

Fanselow, J. (1992). *Contrasting conversations: Activities for exploring our beliefs and teaching practices*. New York: Longman.

Farrell, T. S. C. (2007). *Reflective practice for language teachers: From research to practice*. London: Continuum Press.

Farrell, T. S. C. (2009). *Teaching reading to English language learners: A reflective guide*. Thousand Oaks, CA: Corwin.

Flanders, N. A. (1970). *Analyzing teaching behavior*. Reading, MA: Addison-Wesley.

Forrestal, P. (1990). Talking: Toward classroom action. In M. Brubacher, R. Payne, & K. Rickett (Eds.), *Perspectives on small group learning: Theory and practice* (pp. 158–167). Oakville, Ontario, Canada: Rubicon.

Groisser, P. (1964). *How to use the fine art of questioning*. New York: Teachers' Practical Press.

Hall, E. (1966). *The hidden dimension*. Garden City, NY: Doubleday.

Harmer, J. (1995). Taming the big "I": Teacher performance and student satisfaction. *ELT Journal, 49*(4), 337–345.

Heath, S. B. (1982). *Ways with words: Language, life, and work in communities and classrooms*. New York: McGraw-Hill.

Hurt, T. J., Scott, M. D., & McCroskey, J. C. (1978). *Communication in the classroom*. Reading, MA: Addison-Wesley.

Ivy, D. K., & Backlund, P. (2000). *Exploring genderspeak: Personal effectiveness in gender communication* (2nd ed.). Boston: McGraw-Hill.

Jacobs, G., & Farrell, T. S. C. (2003). Understanding and implementing the CLT (communicative language teaching) paradigm. *RELC Journal, 34*(1), 5–30.

Johnson, K. (1995). *Understanding communication in second language classrooms*. New York: Cambridge University Press.

Knapp, M. L., & Hall, J. A. (1992). *Nonverbal communication in human interaction* (3rd ed.). New York: Holt, Rinehart and Winston.

Lewis, M. (2002). *Giving feedback in language classes*. Singapore: RELC.

McCollum, P. (1989). Turn-allocation in lessons with North American and Puerto Rican students: A comparative study. *Anthropology & Education Quarterly, 20,* 133–157.

McCroskey, L. L., & McCroskey, J. C. (2002). Willingness to communicate and communication apprehension. In J. L. Chesebro & J. C. McCroskey (Eds.), *Communication for teachers* (pp. 19–34). Boston: Allyn & Bacon.

McNeill, D. (1992). *Hand and mind: What gestures reveal about thought*. Chicago: University of Chicago Press.

Mehan, H. (1979). *Learning lessons: Social organization in the classroom*. Cambridge, UK: Cambridge University Press.

Mercer, N. (1995). *The guided construction of knowledge: Talk amongst teachers and learners*. Clevedon, UK: Multilingual Matters.

Neil, S. (1991). *Classroom nonverbal communication (International Library of Psychology)*. New York: Chapman and Hall.

Pennycook, A. (1985). Actions speak louder than words: Paralanguage, communication and education. *TESOL Quarterly, 19,* 259–282.

Philips, S. (1972). Participation structures and communicative competence: Warm Springs children in community and classroom. In C. B. Cazden (Ed.), *Functions of language in the classroom* (pp. 370–394). New York: Teachers College Press.

Philips, S. (1983). *The invisible culture*. New York: Longman Press.

Powell, R., & Caseau, D. (2004). *Classroom communication and diversity: Enhancing instructional practice*. Mahwah, NJ: Lawrence Erlbaum.

Richards, J. C., & Lockhart, C. (1994). *Reflective teaching in second language classrooms*. New York: Cambridge University Press.

Ross, R. S. (1978). *Essentials of speech communication*. Englewood Cliffs, NJ: Prentice Hall.

Rowe, M. B. (1974).Wait-time and rewards as instructional variables, their influence in language, logic and fate control. Part 1: Wait time. *Journal of Research in Science Teaching, 11,* 81–94.

Sadker, D., & Sadker, M. (1994). *Failing at fairness: How our schools cheat girls*. Toronto, Ontario, Canada: Simon & Schuster.

Sinclair, J. M., & Coulthard, M. (1975). *Towards an analysis of discourse: The English used by teachers and pupils*. London: Oxford University Press.

Sinclair, J. M., & Coulthard, M. (1992). Towards an analysis of discourse. In M. Coulthard (Ed.), *Advances in spoken discourse analysis* (pp. 1–34). London: Routledge.

Stevick, E. (1982). *Teaching and learning languages*. New York: Cambridge University Press.

Tsui, A. (1995). *Classroom interaction*. London: Penguin.

Index

Academic task structure, 41–44
Action zones, 87
Active listening, 9
Advice, feedback as, 62
African-American students, 4–5
Analysis of data. *See* Collection and
    analysis of data
Apprehension, 25
Asian students, 13–14
Autonomy (student), 63, 75–76

Back referencing, 43
Barnes, D., 52–53
Biggs, A. P., 18–19
Bloom's Taxonomy, 78

Chicanos, 24
Choice elicitations, 10
Classroom, defined, 7
Classroom communication
    goals of, 8
    as negotiation between students and
        teachers, 11–12, 14, 74–75
    normal communication compared
        with, 7–8, 28–29
    phases of, 42
    reflection on, 95–98
    responsibility for, 12
    student responsibility for, 12
    style, variability of, 29–31
    teacher authority in, 7–8, 10
    See also Nonverbal communication
Classroom communicative
    competence
    apprehension and, 25
    defined, 19

etiquette and, 19–20
gender and, 24–25
home communications and, 21–23
reflection on, 26, 97–98
Classroom observations, 93–94
Closed reasoning questions, 52–53
Collaborative learning, 76–77
Collection and analysis of data
    acknowledgments, 29
    analyzing data, 33–35
    awareness of, 27–28
    collecting of data, 31–32
    cultural background and, 34–35
    IRE sequence, 28
    nonverbal communication, 82, 89
    observations of classrooms and,
        93–94
    recording communications, 31–32
    reflection on, 36
    style, variability of, 29–31
    transcripts, 31–33, 34
    See also Professional Development
Communication
    classroom communication
        compared with, 7–8, 28–29
    constructivist model of, 41
    as contextual, 6
    cultural background, effect on, 3–4
    defined, 5
    low-context vs. high-context, 22–23
    principles of, 6
    questioning as mode of, 4–5
    reflection about, need for, 1
    transmission model of, 41
    See also Classroom communication;
        Nonverbal communication

Competence. *See* Classroom
    communicative competence
Conflict within groups, 79
Constructivist model, 41
Cooperation. *See* Participation
Critical thinking skills, 78
Cultural background
    African-American students, 4–5
    Asian students, 13–14
    Chicanos students, 24
    communication backgrounds and,
        21–23
    effect of, 3–4
    gestures and, 84
    institutionalized racism and, 19
    "I Treat Them All the Same"
        study, 18–19
    low-context vs. high-context
        communication and, 22–23
    proxemics and, 86
    Puerto Rican students, 72–75
    reflection on, 97
    transcripts to gather data and,
        34–35
    Warm Springs Indian Reservation
        students, 21–22

Data. *See* Collection and analysis of
    data
Directive/focused strategy, 9
Display questions, 4–5, 49, 52

Echoic questions, 53–54
Edwards, V., 18–19
Elicit: Agree, 66
Elicitation acts. *See* IRE sequence
Elicit: Confirm, 66
Elicit: Inform, 66
Elicit: Repeat, 67
Epistemic questions, 53–54
Ethnicity. *See* Cultural background
Etiquette, 19–20, 41
Evaluation responses, 28–29
Expectations, 4–5, 95–96. *See also*
    Participation
Exploratory talk, 44–46

Facial expressions, 84–85
Factual (display) questions, 4–5, 49, 52
Feedback
    categories of, 68
    elicitation acts, 10–11, 65–67
    in groups, 78
    language for, 67–68
    OK, meanings of, 64–65
    purposes of, 62–63
    reflection on, 68, 96
    strategies for, 63–68
    student autonomy and, 63
    students' interpretation of, 61
Final draft talk, 44–46
Focused/directive strategy, 9
Focused/nondirective strategy, 9

Gender, 19, 24–25
Gestures, 84
Groupings
    overview, 69–70
    physical setting and, 86–87
    reflection on, 80
    small groups/pairs, 75–77
    success of, fostering, 77–79
    whole-class, 70–75
Guessing questions, 58

Higher-order questions, 53

Iconic gestures, 84
Independent learners. *See* Student
    autonomy
Informant strategies, 50–52
Initiation. *See* IRE sequence
Insight. *See* Collection and
    analysis of data
IRE sequence
    overview, 10–11
    as feedback, 65–67
    as final draft talk, 45
    as limiting students' role,
        33–34
    as structured communication, 28
    student-initiated, 30–31
IRF sequence, 11

"I Treat Them All the Same" (Biggs
    and Edwards), 18–19

Journal writing, 94–95

Kinesics, 83–85

Leading questions, 58
Listening, 9–10. *See also* Nonverbal
    communication
Lockstep groupings (whole-class),
    70–75
Lower cognitive level questions, 53

Marked patterns, 29–31
Metaphoric gestures, 84
Metaprocess elicitations, 11
Mexican-Americans, 24
Motivation, feedback as, 62–63

Native Americans, 21–22
Nondirective/focused strategy, 9
Nonverbal communication
    overview, 81
    collection and analysis of data
        on, 82
    functions of, 82–83
    reflection on, 90, 97
    teachers' use of, 88–90
    types of, 83–87
    Warm Springs Indian Reservation
        children and, 22

Observations of classrooms, 93–94
OK, meanings of, 64–65
Open reasoning questions, 52–53

Pairs and small groups, 75–77
Participation
    academic task structure and,
        41–44
    barriers to, 38–40
    etiquette of, 41
    expectations and, 37
    physical setting and, 86–87
    reflection on, 47

social participation structure and,
        41, 44
    teacher talk and, 44–46
    turn allocation and, 55, 71–75
Patterns, marked, 29–31
Perception checks, 9
Personally qualified strategy, 10
Philips, S., 21–22
Physical setting (proxemics), 86–87
Preformulation questions, 50–51
Process elicitations, 11
Product elicitations, 11
Professional development, 34, 91–97.
        See also Collection and analysis
        of data
Proxemics, 86–87
Puerto Rican students, 72–75

Questions
    awareness about, lack of,
        49–50, 52
    directing of, 55, 71–75
    display questions, 4–5, 49, 52
    good questions, characteristics of,
        56–57
    informant strategies, 50–52
    preformulation questions, 50–51
    reflection on, 60
    reformulation questions, 50–51
    sequencing of, 53, 56–57
    types of, 52–54
    unproductive questions,
        characteristics of, 57–58
    uses for, 49
    wait-time after, 58–59

Race. *See* Cultural background
Record-transcribe-analyze. *See*
        Collection and analysis of data
Reflection
    classroom communication
        data and, 36
    competence and, 26
    expectations and, 95–96
    feedback, purposes of, 68
    groupings and, 80

need for, 1, 13–15
nonverbal communication and, 90
as professional development, 92–95
questions, use of, 60
transcripts for, 47
Reformulation questions, 50–51
Rules, 6

Sadker, D., 25
Sadker, M., 25
Schemata, expectations and, 5
Sequences. *See* IRE sequence; IRF
    sequence
Shy students, 25
Small groups and pairs, 75–77
Social participation structure, 41, 44
Sociofugal arrangements, 86

Sociopetal arrangements, 86
Student autonomy, 63, 75–76

Tag questions, 45
Task structure, academic, 41–44
Teacher talk, 44–46
Transcripts, 31–33, 34
Transmission model, 41
Tugging questions, 58
Turn allocation, 55, 71–75

Wait-time after questions, 58–59
Warm Springs Indian Reservation,
    21–22
Whole-class groupings, 70–75

Yes–no questions, 58